SKILLS Coach
America's Best for Student Success

Open-Ended Questions

Think,
Write,
Assess,
Improve

J

Lida Lim
Margaret C. Moran

Open-Ended Questions Coach, Level J: Read, Think, Write, Assess, Improve
104NA
ISBN# 1-59823-032-8

EVP, Publisher: Steven Zweig
VP, Creative Director: Spencer Brinker
VP of Production: Dina Goren
Executive Editor: Adriana Velez
Art Director: Farzana Razak

Authors: Lida Lim and Margaret C. Moran
Contributing Authors: Corinne Ankenbruck-Keogh, Eric B. Pollock, Rita Read, Mandie Rosenberg

Senior Development Editor: Elizabeth Jaffe
Development Editor: Hank Nourse
Contributing Editor: Lesli J. Favor, Ph.D.
Cover Design: Farzana Razak
Cover Photo: Microzoa/The Image Bank/Getty Images

Triumph Learning® 136 Madison Avenue, 7th Floor, New York, New York 10016
© 2005 Triumph Learning, LLC
A Haights Cross Communications® Inc. Company

Printed in the United States of America.

10 9 8 7 6 5 4 3 2 1

Table of Contents

Unit III   Answering Questions That Ask You to Analyze

Part B

Part A · Introduction

The Smart Way to Answer

Open-Ended Questions!

1 READ
THINK 2
3 WRITE
ASSESS 4
5 IMPROVE

Welcome to the smart way to write answers to open-ended questions!

Do you know how other students answer open-ended questions? Some students dive right in. They read the question and start writing. They never reread the question or plan what they are going to write. They don't even make sure they know what the question is asking. Other students read the question twice. They read it the second time to make sure they understand what it is asking. Then they plan what they're going to say. They may even make some notes or draw some diagrams. Then they start to write.

This is the smart way to answer open-ended questions:

Read · Think · Write · Assess · Improve

Let's look at each step.

1 **READ** the question thoughtfully. Look for key words such as *describe, explain,* and *personal experience.* Key words will help you know what to do.

2 **THINK** about what the reading says, if there is a reading. Think about what the question asks you to write. Brainstorm ideas to answer the question.

3 **WRITE.** Organize your ideas. Now write your answer.

4 **ASSESS** what you have written. *Assess* means to read your writing and see how you might improve it. Ask yourself how you might make your writing answer the question better.

5 **IMPROVE** your writing. Revise your answer as needed. Rework your answer so it responds to the question more *clearly, accurately,* and *completely.*

Going through these 5 steps may seem like a lot of work now. But once you learn the steps, you will see how easy they are to use. This book will help you practice them. By the time you are finished, you will find that you don't even have to think about using the steps. They will come naturally to you. You will read an open-ended question on a test and say to yourself, "Here's an open-ended question. What is the question asking me to do?" And you'll be on your way to applying the 5 steps.

As you will see, these steps work for *any type of open-ended test question.* It doesn't matter if the question is based on a reading or on your personal opinion. It doesn't matter if you have to write a short answer or a long answer. These 5 steps work for all kinds of questions and answers.

Answering Questions That Ask for Information

Lesson 1

Identifying the Main Idea and Supporting Details

The **main idea** of a piece of writing is what the piece is about. It is the topic, or subject, of the piece. The main idea may be expressed directly, or it may be implied. If the main idea is stated directly, you will probably find it within the first paragraph. Often, it is the first sentence of the piece. If the main idea is implied, you will have to figure it out by reading and thinking about what the piece says. In long pieces of writing, the main idea is usually implied rather than stated directly.

Supporting details will help you determine the main idea. **Supporting details** present examples, reasons, facts, statistics, or descriptions that develop and explain the main idea. Some details are more important than others in explaining or describing the main idea. These are **major details**. Less important details are **minor details**. If you have to summarize a piece of writing, use the major details. Do not clutter your summary with minor details. This is true in any writing that requires you to use supporting details to help make your point. Stick to the major details.

Some questions ask about the main idea directly. Others ask about the main idea indirectly. The following are examples of disguised main-idea questions:

- Why is "Moving Day" a good title for this short story?
- Read the interview. Then plan and write an essay explaining Toni Morrison's choice of subject matter for her novels. Use relevant information from the selection to write your essay.
- Read the following two articles on conserving oil resources. Write an essay that combines information from the two articles and explains the authors' views on conservation. Use relevant information in your answer.

None of the questions asks you to write about the main idea and supporting details. However, to answer each question you must find the main idea and supporting details.

In the first question, the title states the main idea of the short story. You then have to identify details in the story that support the writer's choice of title.

The second question asks you to identify and explain Morrison's choice of subject matter. The main idea of the reading must be something about her choice of subjects. The prompt tells you to choose *relevant* supporting details. *Relevant* means *important*. Always use relevant, or major, details whether the prompt reminds you to or not.

In the third question, the main idea of each article must be conservation of oil resources. The details of each article must explain some ideas about oil conservation. To answer the question, you need to pull together details from each article and arrange them in such a way that you explain why the two authors think conservation is important. The third question is similar to the second question except that it asks you to use information from two articles instead of one.

For all three questions, you have to recognize the main idea of the passage. Then you have to use supporting details to explain and describe it to your audience.

When you write, pay attention to the *flow* of your writing, or how easy it is to understand. Does your writing read smoothly and interestingly? Or is your writing filled with short, simple sentences, making it hard for readers to get your point? One way to improve flow is to combine sentences. Taking a series of short, choppy sentences and joining them together into longer sentences is called **sentence combining**.

In this Lesson, you will learn how to...

- answer a question that asks you to use supporting details to write about the main idea.
- choose relevant details.
- make your writing easier to read and more interesting by combining sentences.

TWO HEROES:
CÉSAR CHÁVEZ AND DOLORES HUERTA

Today, César Chávez and Dolores Huerta are considered heroes. They worked tirelessly to improve the working conditions and lives of Mexican-American and Mexican migrant farm workers. However, the two colleagues were not always considered heroes. Until the 1960s, the issues of migrant workers and the workers themselves were ignored by most Americans. Migrant farm workers move from region to region following the seasonal planting and harvesting of crops. The workers had no unions and little legal protection against abusive employers. Employers paid them as little as they could get away with. Chávez and Huerta worked together for more than 30 years in the cause of migrant workers. Their dedication to enacting change through nonviolent means led to many reforms in the working and living conditions of migrant workers.

César Chávez and Dolores Huerta both knew firsthand the problems of migrant workers, and both became activists as a result. Chávez was born in Yuma, Arizona, in 1927. His parents had come from Mexico. When he was a small child, his parents owned a farm. However, they lost it during the Great Depression, when he was ten. The only work Chávez's parents could find was as migrant farm workers. They piled the family into a truck and followed the seasonal pattern of planting, caring for fields, and then harvesting crops. Chávez left school after the eighth grade to work in the fields with the rest of his family.

Dolores Huerta was born in 1930 in Dawson, New Mexico. Her ancestors had been among the first Spanish settlers to come to the Americas in the 1600s. Her father was a migrant farm worker and also worked for a time as a miner. The living and working conditions of miners were no better than those of migrant farm workers. Her father was also an activist, working to improve conditions for his fellow workers. When her parents divorced, Dolores moved to Stockton, California, with her mother and siblings. There, her mother worked and saved, and was able to buy a hotel that rented rooms to farm workers. Huerta learned firsthand from them the problems of migrant workers.

Huerta credits her mother with instilling in her the values of independence and activism. Huerta attended college, which was very unusual for a Hispanic woman at the time. After receiving her teaching certificate, Huerta went to work as a teacher. Her students were mostly the children of migrant workers. Many children did not have shoes or proper clothing. Huerta decided she could have more of an impact by working to improve the lives of migrant workers and their families than by teaching.

Chávez and Huerta met while working for the Community Service Organization (CSO), which was a Hispanic civil rights group. By day, Chávez worked in the fields. After work, he helped register voters for the CSO. Chávez and Huerta founded the National Farm Workers Association (NFWA) in 1962, after the CSO refused to help in a movement to unionize farm workers. The CSO did not believe such a movement would be successful. Chávez and Huerta believed that setting up a union would give farm workers some legal protections against farm owners. A union would also give the workers a single voice to bargain for better wages and working conditions.

In 1965, the Agricultural Workers Organizing Committee (AWOC), made up of Filipino workers, went on strike against grape growers in Delano, California. The NFWA joined the strike in support of the workers. In 1966, the two unions merged, forming the United Farm Workers of America (UFWA). The Delano grape strike lasted five years. Union members picketed stores and asked consumers to boycott, or not to buy, grapes. Chávez led a march to Sacramento, the California state capital, to draw national attention to the cause. Support for the workers grew. The strike led to a nationwide boycott of grapes. Finally the grape growers could not hold out any longer. They agreed to a contract with the union in 1970. It was the first time in history that farm workers had won a contract. In 1974, Chávez and Huerta organized a boycott of wines, lettuce, and table grapes that led to the groundbreaking Agricultural Labor Relations Act. This law recognized the rights of farm workers to unionize.

Chávez was a follower of Mohandas Gandhi and Martin Luther King, Jr., both of whom practiced nonviolent protest. In 1968 during the Delano grape strike, Chávez went on a 25-day hunger strike, refusing to eat anything. His purpose was to make sure that the workers' strike and the movement to unionize migrant workers remained peaceful. He knew that it would be much easier to gain and keep public support for a peaceful movement. Chávez continued his policy of nonviolent protest throughout his life. He went on hunger strikes twice more during unionizing efforts. His policy of nonviolence helped attract the support of politicians and other well-known people to the cause of migrant workers. Robert F. Kennedy called Chávez "one of the heroic figures of our time." During his lifetime, Chávez never made more than $6,000 a year.

Huerta and Chávez continued their careers as activists long after the Delano grape strike. Chávez continued to work for migrant workers until his death in 1993. In 1986, he launched a new campaign that he called the "Wrath of Grapes." Its goal was to alert the public to the dangers to farm workers of pesticides used on farms. Two years later, Chávez went on a 36-day fast, his last, to call attention to the campaign. He was 61 years old. Huerta had joined Chávez in this campaign. Over the years, she had become the top negotiator and lobbyist for "La Causa," the cause for rights for migrant workers.

The cause did not die with Chávez in 1993. Huerta continues her work as an activist. In 1999, she won the Eleanor Roosevelt Award for Human Rights. While working for workers' rights, she also raised a family of 11 children. Huerta's work for migrant workers' rights is even more impressive because she was able to accomplish so much when women were fighting for equal rights for themselves.

STEP 1

READ *the question thoughtfully.*

Read the question carefully.

> **The first sentence of the article states, "Today, César Chávez and Dolores Huerta are considered heroes." The article calls both of them activists. An activist is a person who works directly and aggressively to create political or social change. Identify and describe what these heroes did to change working conditions for migrant workers.**

1. What does the question ask you to do?

   Underline the parts of the question that tell you what to do. These are your key words.

   > **HINT:** *There is a lot of information in this question. Not all of it, however, tells you what to write. Don't underline more than you need to know to answer the question.*

2. **Write those key words here.**

   _____

   _____

3. **Restate in your own words what the question wants you to do.**

   _____

   _____

STEP
2

THINK

THINK about what the biographical sketch says.

1. What is the title of the reading?

    Write the title here.

    _____

2. What does the title tell you the reading is about?

    Write the main idea of the reading here.

    _____

    _____

3. What was the major goal of Chávez and Huerta? Reread the passage if you need to.

    Write the goal here.

    _____

    _____

Skill: Choosing Relevant Details

There is a great deal of information in this biographical sketch about César Chávez and Dolores Huerta. But not all of this information is relevant.

*   How much of the information will help you to answer the question?
*   How much of the information simply makes the sketch more complete and interesting?

For example, that Huerta raised 11 children while working for migrant workers adds interesting information about Huerta the person. But does it add any information about what she did for migrant workers? No; so you would not include this fact in your answer.

4a. How many paragraphs relate to what Chávez and Huerta did for migrant workers?

Put a check mark next to each paragraph that relates to their work. Include paragraphs that are only partly about their work.

4b. **Cross out any information that does not relate directly to their work.**

You have saved yourself a lot of work by narrowing down the information in the sketch to just what you need to develop your answer.

5. Now reread the paragraphs that you checked and look for the details that support Chávez and Huerta's major goal. These are supporting details for your answer.

Write the supporting details here.

_____

_____

_____

_____

_____

_____

_____

THINK about what the question asks you to do.

6. **Write the key words again.**

_____

_____

7. As you see from the list you have generated, Chávez and Huerta did many things to help migrant workers.

   Place a check mark next to the details in number 5, above, that you will use in your answer.

   > **HINT:** *How many details should you use? Look to see how many lines your answer must fill. To fill only 7 lines, you might need only 3 details, BUT those 3 have to be the 3 most important details. To fill 30 lines, you might need 12 to 15 details. Make sure all of those details are relevant.*

STEP 3 WRITE

1. **Restate what you are to write about.**

   _____

   _____

   > **HINT:** *Always be sure your restatement and the question agree. If they don't, reread the question and rethink what you underlined as key words.*

2. Review the details you have selected.

   Number the details in item 5 of Step 2 in the order in which you want to use them.

3. **Write the main idea for the answer you are going to write.**

   _____

   _____

4. Turn your idea into a topic sentence.

   Write your topic sentence here.

   _____

   _____

   _____

5. **Now pull your ideas together and write your answer.**

   _____

   _____

   _____

   _____

   _____

   _____

   _____

   _____

   _____

   _____

   _____

   _____

   _____

STEP 4

ASSESS *what you have written.*

The teacher-evaluators who score the answers to open-ended questions use rubrics. A rubric is an evaluation guide that lists the qualities that teachers should look for as they assess students' answers. Typically, a rubric provides guidance for assessing content, organization, word choice, sentence structure, and the conventions of the English language (grammar, mechanics, and punctuation). Teachers use the rubrics to assess how clear, complete, and accurate students' answers are. Apply the following rubric to your answer to see how teachers use rubrics, and how your writing measures up.

4 = I respond clearly, completely, and accurately to the question.
I include a topic sentence that repeats key words from the question.
I include accurate, relevant supporting details.
I present a well-organized answer that is easy to understand.
I use complete sentences.
I use a variety of sentence constructions and lengths, so the answer is interesting to read.
I have no errors in standard English.

3 = I respond to the question clearly and completely.
I include a topic sentence.
I omit some important details, but those I include are stated accurately.
I present an answer that is organized and understandable.
I use complete sentences.
I have some different types of sentence constructions and lengths, so the writing is somewhat interesting.
I have no errors in standard English.

2 = I respond somewhat to the question.
I do not have a topic sentence.
I include more irrelevant than relevant details.
My answer is not completely organized. Some of it is hard to follow and understand.
I do not always use complete sentences.
My writing is difficult to understand because most sentences are short.
I have numerous errors in standard English.

1 = I do not respond to the question.
I do not have a topic sentence.
I include mostly unimportant and irrelevant details.
My answer is difficult to understand because it is disorganized. Events and details are mixed up.
I use many incomplete sentences.
My writing is choppy.
I have numerous errors in standard English.

How does your answer compare to the rubric? Before you decide, take a look at Kojii's answer that earned a "3." See if you can figure out why his answer got a "3" and not a "4."

Two American heroes, César Chávez and Dolores Huerta, changed the working conditions for migrant workers. They helped to organize the workers into a union in order to fight for better working conditions. Conditions did improve under the leadership of Chávez and Huerta. These changes were accomplished by using nonviolent methods.

Because Chávez's parents were migrant workers, he learned firsthand the horrible conditions they worked under. He became a migrant worker himself after he finished the eighth grade. Huerta had a different early life. She was raised by her mother after her parents divorced. Her mother ran a hotel for migrant workers. Her father was a migrant worker, too. Unlike Chávez, Huerta went to college and earned a degree in teaching. Because she taught migrant children, she was able to see the effects of the horrible working and living conditions on migrant workers. She left teaching to become an activist.

Chávez and Huerta met while working for a Hispanic civil rights group. They both felt a union could get better wages and working conditions. A union could bargain more easily than single workers. Chávez and Huerta founded the National Farm Workers Association in 1962 to unionize farm workers. In 1966 the NFWA merged with another group of migrant farm workers to form the United Farm Workers of America. The other union had started a strike against the Delano grape growers. The new union continued the strike. Chávez and Huerta were strong believers in using nonviolent methods to reach their goals. During this strike, Chávez went on a 25-day hunger strike to keep the strike peaceful. This strike lasted five years. During those five years, union members picketed and called for a boycott of grapes. In order to draw attention to migrant workers, Chávez marched to Sacramento, the capital of California. He got the attention of the California government and the attention of the people of the nation. Chávez and Huerta began a national boycott of grapes. The farmers gave in, and the union got a contract.

UFWA began another strike and boycott and got the Agricultural Labor Relations Act passed. This act recognized the right of migrant workers to unionize and fight for better working conditions. Chávez had two more hunger strikes to make people aware of problems migrant workers faced. They protested pesticides that hurt farm workers.

The activism of Chávez and Huerta changed the life of migrant workers for the better. César Chávez and Dolores Huerta are true heroes.

What would an evaluator say about Kojii's answer?
- ✔ He did not read the question carefully, because his answer gives more than the question asks for.
- ✔ He repeats some of the key words from the question in his topic sentence, but he does not limit his answer to just the key words.
- ✔ He supports his answer with details from the reading.
- ✔ He organizes his answer so that each thought is complete and easy to follow.
- ✔ He writes complete sentences.
- ✔ He uses a variety of sentence constructions and lengths, so the answer is interesting to read.

Let's examine Kojii's answer to see why it merits a "3" and not a "4."

1. Kojii repeats some of the key words from the question in his topic sentence.

    Write his topic sentence here.

    _____

    _____

2. What key words does Kojii include in his topic sentence?

    Write the key words that he uses in his topic sentence.

    _____

3. **Write one of Kojii's sentences that tells what Chávez and Huerta did to change conditions for migrant workers.**

    _____

    _____

    _____

4. **Write another sentence from Kojii's answer that describes how Chávez and Huerta worked to help migrant workers.**

    _____

    _____

    _____

5. Have you figured out why Kojii didn't get a "4"? He wrote a paragraph about Chávez's and Huerta's early lives. It's interesting information, but does it help answer the question?

    Restate here what the question asks Kojii to write about.

    _____

    _____

6. What should Kojii do in order to improve his score?

   Write your suggestion(s) here.

   _____

   _____

   _____

One reason that Kojii's answer scored a "3" is because it is interesting to read. He uses a variety of sentence constructions and lengths.

Skill: Combining Sentences

A variety of sentence lengths and constructions makes writing more interesting to read. Short, simple sentences can be boring, and they can make the writer's ideas seem unclear to readers. Likewise, writing that lacks transition words, such as *because, as a result, compared to,* and *unlike,* can be difficult to understand. **Combining sentences** adds interest to a piece of writing and can make the writing easier to understand.

There are a number of ways to combine short sentences into longer ones.
- Use a coordinating conjunction (*and, but, or*) and a comma to combine two sentences.

   During those five years, union members picketed. They called for a boycott of grapes.

   BECOMES

   During those five years, union members picketed and called for a boycott of grapes.

- Use a conjunction and a comma to make one sentence a subordinate clause.

   Chávez's parents were migrant workers. He learned firsthand the horrible conditions they worked under.

   BECOMES

   Because Chávez's parents were migrant workers, he learned firsthand the horrible conditions they worked under.

- Turn the predicate in one sentence into a participle, and make it a subordinate clause.

  In 1966 the NFWA merged with another group of farm workers. They formed the United Farm Workers of America.

  BECOMES

  In 1966 the NFWA merged with another group of farm workers, forming the United Farm Workers of America.

7a. How did Kojii combine these two sentences?

  The farmers gave in. The union got a contract.

  Explain here how Kojii combined these sentences.

  _____

  _____

  _____

7b. Kojii combined these two sentences into one that reads more smoothly.

  They both felt that a union would help migrant workers. Unions could get better wages and working conditions.

  Write the new sentence that Kojii made.

  _____

  _____

  _____

Reread your own answer. Would it read more smoothly and be easier to understand if you combined some sentences? When you revise your answer, consider mixing long and short sentences.

Now let's take a look at your answer.

8. Did you repeat part of the question in your topic sentence?

   If not, rewrite your topic sentence using keywords.

   _____

   _____

   _____

9. Kojii uses 11 relevant details to explain how Chávez and Huerta changed the working conditions of migrant workers. This number does not include the details he uses about their lives. How many relevant details do you have in your answer?

   Write the number here. _____

10. Do you have any details that are not relevant to your topic? Do you include information that is not related to the work that Chávez and Huerta did?

   Reread your answer. Cross out any details that are not necessary to explain the main idea.

11. If you have fewer than 8 relevant details, what details could you add? Go back and read the article again to find more details.

   Write new details here.

   _____

   _____

   _____

   _____

   _____

   _____

   HINT: *To decide whether a detail is relevant, ask yourself,*
   Is this information necessary to explain the main idea?

12. Are most of your sentences simple, short sentences?

    Circle Yes or No.

13. If you circled "Yes," combine some of these sentences when you revise your answer.

    Put brackets around sentences that you could combine.

STEP 5

IMPROVE *your answer.*

1. Think about the ideas you wrote when you assessed your answer.

2. Read the rubric on pages 18–19 again. Think about your answer and about the description of a "4" paper.

3. **Use your new ideas to revise and rewrite your answer here.**

_____

_____

_____

_____

_____

_____

_____

_____

_____

_____

_____

_____

_____

_____

_____

_____

Remember to review the "One Last Look" questions below.

ONE LAST *LOOK*

Did you
❑ answer the question that was asked?
❑ include details to make your answer interesting and complete?
❑ write complete sentences?
❑ fill all or most of the answer lines?
❑ check your spelling and punctuation?

Lesson 2

Identifying a Problem and Its Solution

An open-ended test question may ask you to identify a problem and its solution. For example, you may be asked to identify the problem described in a reading and the solution that is offered in the reading. Or you may be asked to identify the problem described in a reading and then offer your own solution.

If a question asks you about a problem and solution that are directly stated, you should
- identify the stated problem.
- identify the stated solution(s).
- present the details that justify the solution (or best possible solution of several).

If you must provide your own solution to a stated problem, you should
- identify the stated problem.
- present a possible solution.
- present details that justify your solution.
- present a call to action, if one is needed to answer the question completely.

A **call to action** is a request for the audience to do something—to act on the solution. Not all problem-solution questions ask for a call to action, so read the question carefully to see exactly what you are required to write.

How do you go about answering a problem-solution question? If you have a reading selection to work with, you should
- find the paragraph in the selection that describes the problem.
- find the paragraph(s) that present the solution, or possible solutions.
- find the paragraph(s) that present details that justify the solution(s).

Not all problem-solution questions are based on a reading selection. A question may state a problem and ask you to develop a solution based on
- the information stated in the prompt, or question

    AND

- your own experience.

When you write and revise your answer, think about the structure of your sentences. Too many short sentences make your writing choppy. To make your answer read more smoothly, combine short, choppy sentences into longer sentences. However, be careful not to create run-on sentences. You may also find that some of your short sentences aren't really sentences, but sentence fragments. This lesson will help you learn to avoid both sentence fragments and run-on sentences.

In this Lesson, you will learn how to...

- answer an open-ended question, based on two news articles, that asks you to identify a problem and develop a solution.
- combine sentences to avoid run-on sentences and sentence fragments.

NEW HIGHWAY TO BE BUILT THROUGH KARVILLE

Karville—The state legislature has recently announced plans to build a new highway through Karville in Kalamassas County. Construction on the 3-year project will begin next year, and the funding will come from state construction bonds.

Supporters of the highway believe it will solve a number of problems that have plagued Karville since the late 1960s. The new highway would provide residents with a direct link to both Interstate 100 to the west and Interstate 67 to the east. The lack of a direct connection has been a problem for commuters for more than 40 years. Lack of interstate access has also made Karville less attractive to prospective homebuyers. Advocates believe the highway will help revitalize the city by attracting new families to the area. This would, in turn, raise property values for homes of current residents.

Sounds like a good plan, right? So why are some Karville residents protesting the highway?

The major reason that residents are protesting the highway is that it would be built right through East Karville, and more than 100 homes are to be torn down to make room for the highway. The policy of eminent domain gives the government the right to take land necessary for public use. The state legislature has concluded that the benefits from the new highway will far outweigh the loss of homes in East Karville. Residents will receive the fair-market-value price from the government for their land.

As one might imagine, this issue has East Karville residents steaming mad. "Fair-market value!" says Fran Schuler. "How can you place a value on a home? On a neighborhood? I think it is outrageous that the government thinks it can just pay us off and take our land. How will it help our city if we're gone?"

East Karville councilman Jeff Johnson is determined to fight the highway if it is constructed as currently planned. "Clearly, there are more realistic and less invasive solutions to the problem of building a highway in Karville. East Karville is a wonderful, close-knit neighborhood. It adds immeasurably to the character of Karville as a whole. Demolishing homes is just not an option, as far as I am concerned. I don't want to see any of Karville's vital neighborhoods destroyed."

Mr. Johnson continued, "Members of the council would be happy to meet with state representatives and Mayor McKenna to design a more equitable solution to the problem of where to build the highway. No one on the council opposes the building of the highway. We just oppose the unnecessary destruction of a neighborhood."

Karville Mayor Sam McKenna supports the plan to build the highway through East Karville. He did not return calls asking for a comment for this article.

East Karville resident Randy Mastro has been working with Mr. Johnson to identify alternate sites for the highway. "We believe the highway could be most easily built on what is actually government land," he said. "The highway could best be built where the abandoned railroad tracks run through town. No homes or businesses remain on the land surrounding the tracks. Also, the tracks literally split Karville in half, east and west. Building a highway in this location would give people living on both sides of Karville equal access to the highway."

Mr. Mastro continued, "There is another possible route. The highway could be built in a 'half-loop' style around the west side of the city, where there is vacant land. We fail to understand why the state legislature did not investigate these two options."

When asked for comment, a representative of the state legislature did not mention the proposal by Councilman Johnson and his allies. Instead, the representative said that after long consideration, the East Karville site was chosen because it would be the least damaging to the environment around Karville. Mr. Mastro responded, "That's nonsense. The homes in East Karville *are* part of the environment."

Long-time Karville resident Molly Grier sees a different problem with the highway. She does not want *any* highway built in Karville. "The highway won't solve problems," she said. "It will only cause more. A highway would destroy our quiet way of life. Everyone keeps talking about revitalizing the city and bringing in new people, but many of us are quite happy with Karville the way it is. We like it quiet. We don't mind driving on secondary roads to reach the interstates. If we wanted to live near an interstate, we would not live in Karville." Molly Grier offers this solution to the highway-placement problem: "Just don't build a highway. Problem solved!"

33

KARVILLE MAYOR DEFENDS HIGHWAY AT PUBLIC MEETING

Karville—During a sometimes angry public meeting last night, Mayor Sam McKenna of Karville defended the plan to demolish homes in East Karville to make room for the new highway. City Hall's council chambers were packed with opponents of the highway and a surprising number of supporters. After weeks of refusing to comment on the issue, the mayor agreed to a public meeting to calm residents. As his office spokesperson put it, there is a need "to set residents straight on why it is necessary to go forward with the highway plan as it is."

The mayor began the meeting by facing the problem head-on. "No one wants to see people lose their homes," he said. "However, the benefits of the highway are so great that I feel we had no choice but to support the state's plan."

According to the mayor, the plan's benefits include an increase in Karville's population due to the new highway. Increasing the population, the mayor said, would have "a wide-ranging, good effect on Karville. First, an increase in residents will raise property values. Second, more residents will provide Karville with a larger tax base. Third, with a larger tax base, Karville will have more money to invest in revitalization projects. Fourth, the additional tax dollars will benefit our most precious Karville residents—our children. Greater tax dollars mean more funding for our schools, which many of you know are in great need of funds."

Mayor McKenna went on to say, "We plan to put a toll booth on the highway bridge over the Karville River. The state highway commission has already agreed to this, and we'll split the toll monies with the state. The tolls will provide Karville with an estimated one million dollars a year to invest in our schools."

Jennifer Jack, a Karville resident, responded to the mayor. "How do you justify not only forcing some Karville residents from their homes, but charging other Karville residents to use the road?"

The mayor responded, "Let me be clear on this. Karville residents will not have to pay bridge tolls. We are already working with an electronics outfitter to supply special electronic tags that will allow residents to pass through toll booths without paying. All nonresidents will be required to pay the tolls."

"And how, exactly, will that work for those 'former,' future homeless residents of Karville?" responded Jennifer Jack.

The mayor expressed his "deepest concern for those citizens," acknowledging that giving up their homes for a new highway is difficult. He said, "My staff and I have been working overtime to find a way to compensate these people. With the state's help, we've come up with a plan to build a new housing development. There will be homes available for all the displaced families, plus an additional 1,000 families we expect to move to Karville after the completion of the highway. All the former East Karville residents will be given first crack at choosing the housing lots they want. The city will pay half the cost of the new housing and will also arrange low-interest mortgages."

Fran Schuler, another Karville opponent of the highway, asked where the displaced residents would live until the new houses were completed. The mayor responded, "All displaced residents will be settled into their new homes before we break ground on the new highway project."

Councilman Jeff Johnson asked the mayor about the two alternate routes that he was promoting. The mayor responded, "If we said "no" to the state, the state could take the land anyway. I felt it was better to cooperate by agreeing to the

state's plan. By cooperating, we got some things we wanted from the state such as the toll booths on the bridge and help with the new housing development."

At the meeting's conclusion, Karville residents remained divided over the highway issue. A few appeared to have been swayed by the mayor's arguments. Bill Jankelow, an East Karville resident, said, "Well, it's nice to know the mayor actually has a plan to help us folks who will lose our homes. Even if I don't agree with the plan, I feel better knowing that it was thought out."

Another East Karville resident, Joe Anderson, disagreed. "I appreciate the work the mayor and his people have done about finding us new homes. But if I wanted a new home, I would have moved to one on my own. Hard work aside, I think the mayor should go back to the drawing board. There has to be some other way."

Will the new highway be built as planned? Only time will tell.

STEP 1

READ *the question thoughtfully.*

Read the question carefully.

The state is planning to build a new highway through Karville, and this issue has divided the city's residents. You have read two articles about the issue, printed in local newspapers. Using relevant information from both articles, identify the problem and the best solution for the problem.

1. What does the question ask you to do?

   Underline the parts of the question that tell you what to do. These are your key words.

   HINT: *The question gives facts about the articles that you do not need to answer the question. Cross out the information that you don't need. Now underline the key words in what's left.*

2. **Write the key words here.**

   _____

   _____

3. **Restate in your own words what the question asks you to do.**

   _____

   _____

   HINT: *Always check your restatement against the question before you continue.*

STEP 2 THINK

THINK about what the two articles say.

1. Find the paragraph or paragraphs in each article that describe the problem.

   Put a check mark next to the paragraphs.

   Put a bracket around the main statement of the problem in each article.

2. **Write the main problem stated in each article here.**

   Article 1:

   _____

   _____

   Article 2:

   _____

   _____

3. Find the paragraphs in each article that present possible solutions.

   Put an X next to the paragraphs.

4. **Write the possible solutions here.**

   Article 1:

   1. _____

      _____

   2. _____

      _____

   3. _____

   Article 2:

   1. _____

      _____

   2. _____

      _____

5. Find the details that support the solutions you listed in number 4.

   Underline the details for each solution.

   Number each set of details to match the solution (1, 2, or 3).

THINK about what the question asks you to do.

6. **Write the key words again.**

   _____

   _____

7. **Restate what you are to write about.**

   _____

   _____

8. Which do you think is the best solution?

   Write that solution here.

   _____

   _____

9. Find the details that justify, or support, that solution.

   Write those details here.

   _____

   _____

   _____

   _____

   _____

   _____

STEP 3 WRITE

1. **Restate what you are to write about.**

   _____

   _____

2. What is the problem presented in the articles?

   Write the problem here.

   _____

   _____

3. Use your statement of the problem to write your topic sentence.

   Write your topic sentence here.

   _____

   _____

   _____

HINT: *Be sure to repeat some of the key words from the question in your topic sentence. Repeating them helps you stay focused on what you are to write about.*

4. Review the details you listed in Step 2 for the solution you selected.

   Number the details in the order in which you want to use them.

5. **Now write your answer.**

_____

_____

_____

_____

_____

_____

_____

_____

_____

_____

_____

_____

_____

_____

_____

_____

_____

_____

_____

STEP 4

ASSESS *what you have written.*

The answers to open-ended questions are evaluated against a rubric. A rubric is a guide that lists the things to look for in a piece of writing. Apply the following rubric to your answer to see how your writing measures up.

4 = I respond clearly, completely, and accurately to the question.
I include a topic sentence that repeats key words from the question.
I state the problem clearly.
I state the solution to the problem clearly and accurately.
I include details to describe the problem and the solution.
I present a well-organized answer. Planning is evident.
I write complete, grammatically correct sentences.

3 = I respond to the question accurately.
I include a topic sentence, but I use few key words from the question.
I state the problem accurately.
I state a solution to the problem, but it is not completely clear.
I include some details to describe the problem and the solution.
I present a somewhat organized answer.
I write sentences that are for the most part complete and correct.

2 = I do not answer the question completely.
I do not have a topic sentence.
I state the problem and a solution, but not clearly or completely.
Most of the details I use do not help explain the solution.
I have some sentence fragments or run-on sentences.
I make numerous errors in standard English.

1 =   I do not answer the question.
I do not have a topic sentence.
I do not state the problem correctly.
I do not state a solution.
I have written a disorganized answer. No planning is evident.
I have many sentence fragments or run-on sentences.
I make numerous errors in standard English.

How does your answer measure up to the rubric? Before you decide, take a look at Tenaye's answer that earned a "4."

Where to build a new highway is the problem facing the residents of Karville. The state has proposed building the new highway through East Karville. The new highway will link two interstates. The route that has been chosen is creating a lot of controversy.

The proposed route will displace people from East Karville. More than 100 homes will be torn down to make way for the highway. The mayor and other advocates say that the benefits of the new highway are worth displacing people. They claim the problem cannot be solved any other way.

Opponents have identified two other routes for the new highway. These routes do not go through Karville. In fact, neither route would disrupt or destroy any neighborhood in Karville. One route would use the land around the abandoned railroad tracks that run right through the middle of Karville. The land surrounding the tracks is not being used for homes or businesses. Also, building the new highway there

43

will give all residents the same access to the new highway. The other route takes the highway around the west side of the city.

The best solution is to build the highway where the abandoned railroad tracks are. The fewest people will be affected. It seems to be a ready-made solution to this problem. The mayor, state representatives, and those who have proposed the alternate route should meet and agree to use this route. Then the problem facing the residents of Karville will be solved.

What would an evaluator notice about Tenaye's answer?

✔ She must have read the question carefully because she wrote about what it asked.

✔ She repeats some of the key words from the question in her topic sentence.

✔ She states the problem and describes the solution clearly, completely, and accurately.

✔ She uses details to explain the problem and solution.

✔ She writes complete, correct sentences.

Let's examine Tenaye's answer to see why it merits a "4."

1. Tenaye clearly states the problem the city is facing.

   Write the sentence that states the problem.

   _____

   _____

2. Tenaye includes details describing the problem.

   Write one of Tenaye's sentences with a detail about the problem.

   _____

   _____

3. Which solution from the articles does Tenaye select as the best?

   Write the solution that she chooses.

   _____

   _____

4. Tenaye includes details describing the solution.

   Write one sentence with a detail that justifies her choice of solutions.

   _____

   _____

One reason that Tenaye's answer scores a "4" is that she writes complete sentences. She has no run-on sentences or sentence fragments.

Skill: Revising Run-on Sentences and Sentence Fragments

A **run-on sentence** is made up of two or more complete sentences joined without proper punctuation or conjunctions. That punctuation may be a comma, period, question mark, colon, or semicolon. The conjunction could be *and, but, while, although,* or another similar word. A **sentence fragment** is an incomplete sentence. It lacks a subject or a predicate. A writer may make both kinds of mistakes while hurrying to get his or her ideas down on paper.

To correct a run-on sentence,
* use a period and a capital letter.
* use a conjunction and a comma, if needed.

Write Tenaye's revision of each run-on sentence below.

5a. The state has proposed building the new highway through East Karville, the new highway will link two interstates.

   _____

   _____

   _____

5b. One route would use the land around the abandoned railroad tracks, they run right through the middle of Karville.

_____

_____

_____

To revise a sentence fragment, first determine whether the fragment is missing a **subject** (who or what the sentence is about) or a **predicate** (what the subject is or does). Then,

- add a subject, if needed.
- add a predicate, if needed.

Write Tenaye's revision of each sentence fragment below.

5c. More than 100 homes will be torn down. To make way for the highway.

_____

_____

5d. Also will give all residents the same access to the new highway.

_____

_____

Reread your own answer. Do you have any run-on sentences or sentence fragments? If you do, be sure to correct them when you revise your answer.

Now let's take a look at your answer.

6. Do you state the problem clearly?

If not, write a sentence that states the problem here.

_____

_____

_____

7. Would adding details make the problem clearer to the reader?

   If yes, write additional details here.

   _____

   _____

   _____

8. Do you state your choice of solution clearly and completely?

   If not, rewrite your statement of the solution clearly and completely.

   _____

   _____

   _____

9. Should you add more details to make your chosen solution more clear and complete?

   If yes, write additional details here.

   _____

   _____

   _____

10. Do you have any sentence fragments or run-on sentences?

    Circle any sentence fragments that you need to revise.

    Put brackets around any run-on sentences that you need to revise.

STEP 5

IMPROVE *your answer.*

1. Think about the ideas you have written down about your answer.

2. Read the rubric on pages 42–43 again. Think about your answer and about the description of a "4" paper.

3. **Use your new ideas to revise and rewrite your answer.**

_____

_____

_____

_____

_____

_____

_____

_____

_____

_____

_____

_____

_____

_____

_____

_____

_____

_____

_____

_____

Remember to review the "One Last Look" questions below.

ONE LAST LOOK

Did you

❏ answer the question that was asked?
❏ include details to make your answer interesting and complete?
❏ write complete sentences?
❏ fill all or most of the answer lines?
❏ check your spelling and punctuation?

Lesson 3

Identifying and Describing a Personal Experience, Part 1

A **personal narrative** describes a personal experience. In a personal narrative, you can write about your comical aunt, a great CD you just heard, a frightening experience you had, or the best or worst day in your life. A personal essay can be about anything that affected you or that you were a part of.

On a test, an open-ended question might ask you to write about
- a skill, hobby, or interest that you have.
- the main idea of an essay and how it relates to your own life.
- a central theme in a poem or story and how it relates to your own life.
- an experience that you have had that is similar to one in the selection.

Sometimes you may be asked to write about someone else's experience. For instance, the question may ask you to write about the experience of a friend or a literary character. But in this lesson, you will relate the main idea of the reading selection to your own life.

You will plan your essay by answering these six planning questions:
✔ **What** is the event I will write about?
✔ **Who** was involved?
✔ **Where** did the experience take place?
✔ **When** did it take place?
✔ **How** did it turn out? That is, how did the experience affect me?
✔ **Why** did it turn out the way it did?

To make your answer interesting to the reader, be sure to include **descriptive details**. These are words and phrases that help your reader "see" what you are writing about. As a result, your writing will be more interesting and easier to understand.

In this Lesson, you will learn how to...
- answer a question that asks you to describe a personal experience.
- use descriptive details to make your answer more interesting.

ACHIEVING MY GOALS

by Eric B. Pollock

I may be a high school student, but I have already learned some important lessons about achievement. Through my experiences so far in life, I have learned a simple but important rule: Through hard work and determination, a person can achieve success.

I have learned that persistence pays off, cooperation leads to success, and using my potential to the fullest will achieve my goals. Every accomplishment I have achieved so far has been the result of these qualities working in harmony. They have helped me to adapt to change and to overcome new obstacles as they came up. I strongly believe that anyone with these qualities will reach great heights. I know I will in my life because of them. This is not bragging. It is the result of my experiences.

At a very young age, I learned the quality of persistence and how it can lead to success. I was nine years old when I took my first piano lesson. For the next six years, I learned the truth of the old saying "practice makes perfect." Persistence is what carried me through the rough times when I thought a piece was too difficult or too long to learn. I also saw the direct relationship between persistence and success. When I skipped practice, it was reflected in my lessons. The more I practiced, the more natural my playing became. Persistence in practicing and working through the difficulties of various pieces helped me achieve a level in playing that I never dreamed of when I took my first lesson. I now know the power of persistence and what I am able to achieve because of it.

Hard work is a very general term, but being able to work hard is another important quality that leads to success. In the winter of my eighth-grade year, I eagerly took a job as a busboy in a very fast-paced restaurant. This job taught me about the speed and accuracy you need in a work situation. I learned about what makes great customer relations. I learned to become more aware of specific customer needs and wants. Above all I learned that even for a busboy, there is no room for error, and that everyone needs to cooperate and work together to keep the operation running smoothly. One error in the workplace can affect the efficiency of all people who work there.

I have tried a variety of sports, but wrestling is my passion. Success in wrestling is based on an individual's willingness to work and drive to new levels of endurance and skill. I earned my varsity spot through persistence and hard work. I pushed myself harder and harder in physical training and in practice. It is my self-motivation and drive that has helped me master both the mental and physical aspects of the sport. Through wrestling I have discovered that individuals possess unlimited potential. Just when I thought I could

51

not push myself more, I would always find a new level of intensity and hard work. Every time I step on the mat, I bring with me total concentration. Because of this, I reached the state finals as a sophomore. It is this same attitude that I direct to all the important aspects of my life, whether it is family relationships, friendships, schoolwork, or a job.

My work ethic enables me to take on any task whether it be difficult or menial. My work ethic is a direct result of how I was raised and how I set my values. My parents have always told me that nothing comes easily. However, with persistence and a determined mindset, you will come out on top. Through my work experience, I have found that as part of a team, with great cooperation, you can achieve great success. Lastly, through athletics I have found that with the right attitude and understanding of myself, I reached heights to which my abilities alone could not have taken me. My work ethic not only defines my abilities and the depth of my potential, but it defines who I am and how I choose to live my life.

STEP 1

READ *the question thoughtfully.*

Read the question carefully.

In the essay, Eric writes, "Through my experiences so far in life, I have learned a simple but important rule: Through hard work and determination, a person can achieve success." So far in your life, what have you learned about achieving goals? Write a well-organized answer that describes a goal that you set for yourself and achieved. Include details about how you achieved your goal and how achieving the goal has affected your life.

1. What does the question ask you to do?

   Underline the parts of the question that tell you what to do. These are your key words.

2. **Write those key words here.**

   _____

   _____

3. **Restate in your own words what the question asks you to do.**

   _____

   _____

HINT: *How do you know if your restatement is correct? Check it against the question.*

THINK about what the essay describes.

1. What is the title of the essay?

   Write the title here.

   _____

2. What is the main idea of the essay?

   Write the main idea here.

   _____

   _____

This is the answer to the first planning question, _What am I going to write about?_
Does the writer remember to answer the other five planning questions in writing
his essay?

3. **_Who_ besides himself does the writer talk about in his essay?**

   _____

4. **What places—the _where_—does the writer mention?**

   _____

5. **_When_ do the events, or experiences, take place?**

   _____

6. *How* did these experiences turn out? That is, how did they affect the writer?

_____

_____

_____

> **HINT:** *The writer states that he learned three qualities from his experiences. What are those three qualities? Focusing on those qualities will help you to answer questions 6 and 7.*

7. *Why* did the writer's experiences turn out the way they did? In other words, why did he come to believe these qualities are so important?

   Write what the writer learned about these three qualities.

_____

_____

_____

THINK about what the question asks you to do.

8. **Write the key words again.**

_____

_____

Now use the six planning questions to help you plan and organize your essay.

9. *What* is the achievement you want to write about? Do you want to write about

   - an academic achievement?
   - an athletic achievement?
   - an achievement that showed skill?
   - an achievement that showed responsibility?
   - an achievement that showed maturity?

   Circle the type of achievement you are going to write about.

10. **Write the actual achievement that you are going to write about.**

_____

_____

The next step in planning is to brainstorm the details that you will need to support and describe your main idea. You will need to include details that create a "picture" for your reader.

Skill: Using Descriptive Details

Descriptive details are details that help your reader "see" what you are writing about. Good descriptive writing includes vivid adjectives and adverbs, and action verbs. It also includes lots of information.

The writer of the essay could have written the following:

> When I was an eighth grader, I worked in a restaurant.

Instead, he wrote:

> In the winter of my eighth-grade year, I eagerly took a job as a busboy in a very fast-paced restaurant.

Which sentence creates a picture for you of

- what the writer did and felt?
- where he was?
- what the place was like?

11a. The writer talks about his piano playing. He could have written,

> Persistence got me through those times that were tough.

Find the sentence he wrote instead, and write it here.

_____

_____

11b. The writer uses nine sentences to describe his experiences wrestling.

Write five words or phrases that he uses to describe how he felt, what he did, and what he learned from wrestling.

_____

_____

_____

_____

_____

As you plan your answer, be sure to brainstorm words and phrases that describe how you felt, what you did, and what you learned as you achieved your goal.

Now, begin your brainstorming. The more information you write down now, the easier it will be to write a complete draft.

12. **Who was involved in achieving your goal?**

_____

_____

13. **Where did you achieve this goal?**

_____

_____

14. **When did the experience take place?**

_____

_____

15. *How* did the experience turn out? That is, how did it affect your life?

_____

_____

_____

_____

16. *Why* did it turn out the way it did?

_____

_____

_____

_____

17. Think about the experience you are going to write about. Reread the answers to your planning questions in numbers 10 and 12–16. Do you need more details to help fill out what happened?

   Add more details where they are needed in numbers 12–16.

STEP 3

WRITE

1. **Restate what you are to write about.**

   _____

   _____

2. Use the achievement you selected to write your topic sentence.

   Write your topic sentence here.

   _____

   _____

3. Review your answers to the six planning questions (items 10 and 12–16 of Step 2).

   Number them in the order in which you want to use them.

   > **HINT:** *As you write your answer to the open-ended question, remember to use descriptive details. Remember, too, that the details have to be relevant to your topic.*

4. **Now write your answer.**

   _____

   _____

   _____

   _____

   _____

_____

_____

_____

_____

_____

_____

_____

_____

_____

_____

STEP
4

ASSESS *what you have written.*

Apply the following rubric to your answer to see what an evaluator will be looking for and how your answer measures up.

4 =   I answer the question clearly, completely, and accurately.
      I include a topic sentence that repeats key words from the question.
      I include supporting details that create a picture of the event.
      I present a well-organized answer. Planning is evident.
      I use complete and correct sentences.

3 =   I answer the question accurately, but not completely.
      I include a topic sentence with some key words from the question.
      I use details that for the most part support the main idea.
      I develop the details using some description.
      I present a somewhat organized answer.
      I use complete and correct sentences.

2 =   I do not answer the question completely or clearly.
      I do not have a topic sentence.
      I include a few supporting details.
      I do not include enough description to help the reader "see" the event.
      I include many unnecessary details.
      I make numerous errors in standard English.

1 =   I do not answer the question.
      I do not have a topic sentence.
      I include many irrelevant details and little description.
      I present a disorganized answer. No planning is evident.
      I make numerous errors in standard English.

How does your answer compare to the rubric? Before you decide, take a look at Armando's answer. It scored a "4."

During the summer when I was 12, I learned that fulfilling a responsibility was a way to achieve a goal, and was part of growing up, too. I wanted a new dirt bike. My parents agreed, if I could pay for half.

I was trying to figure out how I would earn the money when I saw a flier at the rec center. The local newspaper was looking for people to deliver papers every morning. The route in my neighborhood was available, so I called. A week later, I began my paper route.

I had to pick up my papers and delivery addresses at a specific corner. The stack of newspapers was huge. I sat at the curb and folded the papers, stuffed them into my news bag, hooked the bag onto my bike, and off I went. I rode to the front of the first house and tossed the paper. It landed neatly in front of the door. How easy! I saw the money rolling in. That morning and the following morning were perfect. Without a doubt, I was the best newsboy in the city.

The third day was a different story. It was raining. I got to the pick-up place and my newspapers were covered in plastic. There was also a big bundle of plastic bags. I had to take it all home. In the garage, I put each paper in a plastic bag. It seemed to take forever.

By the time I started my route, it was over two hours later than usual. Many of my customers had already called the newspaper to complain. After I finished, there was a message at home to call my supervisor. She was not happy. She told me that on rainy days I had to pick up my papers much earlier so I could get my route completed on time.

It stormed all that night. The next day was rainy and windy. I got to the pick-up place two hours early. I was so sleepy that I thought I was sleepwalking. I took the papers home, bagged them, and started my route. The wind made it hard to ride my bike. It also sent my papers flying all over. I had to stop at each house and walk the paper to the door. I knew customers would not want to go out in the rain to get their paper. It took me a little longer, but not much. I was dreading a phone call from my supervisor. No call came. I had fulfilled my responsibility.

I kept that job for two years and earned more than enough money to get my dirt bike. I achieved my goal. Along the way, I learned the importance of being responsible about doing your job.

Why do you think that Armando's answer scored a "4"?

- ✔ He must have read the question carefully because he wrote about what it asks.
- ✔ He repeats some of the key words from the question in his topic sentence.
- ✔ He uses many details to support his main idea.
- ✔ He uses many descriptive details to develop his main idea.
- ✔ He writes complete sentences.

Let's examine Armando's answer to see why it earned a "4."

1. Armando repeats some of the key words from the question in his topic sentence.

    Write those key words here.

    _____

2. Armando identifies his main idea in his topic sentence. It answers the question, *What* will I write about?

    Write Armando's topic sentence here.

    _____

    _____

Now answer the other five planning questions based on Armando's answer.

3. ***Who* is involved?**

    _____

4. ***Where* does the experience take place?**

    _____

5. ***When* does it take place?**

    _____

6. ***How* does it turn out? How is Armando affected by the experience?**

    _____

    _____

7. ***Why* does it turn out the way it does?**

    _____

    _____

8. Armando develops his main idea by using descriptive details.

   Write three of those details here.

   _____

   _____

   _____

Now evaluate your answer. How does it measure up to Armando's? Do you paint a picture for readers the way Armando does?

9. Did you use some key words from the question in your topic sentence?

   If not, rewrite your topic sentence using some of those key words.

   _____

   _____

   _____

10. Is your essay missing any of the *who, where, when, why,* and *how* of the *what* the achievement you wrote about? If yes, what did you forget to include?

    Write what you forgot to include.

    _____

    _____

    _____

    _____

    _____

11. Would adding more description help readers to better "see" and understand what happened? If yes, what descriptive details could you add?

Write additional descriptive details here.

_____

_____

_____

_____

_____

_____

12. Did you write only complete sentences? Reread your answer.

Underline any sentence fragments or run-on sentences, and rework them when you revise your answer.

13. Would your answer be stronger if you combined short sentences?

Put brackets around any sentences you could combine in your revision.

STEP
5

IMPROVE *your answer.*

1. Think about the ideas you wrote as you assessed your answer.

2. Read the rubric on page 62 again. Think about your answer and about the description of a "4" paper.

3. **Use your new ideas to revise and rewrite your answer.**

_____

_____

_____

_____

_____

_____

_____

_____

_____

_____

_____

_____

_____

_____

_____

_____

Remember to review the "One Last Look" questions below.

ONE LAST
LOOK

Did you
❏ answer the question that was asked?
❏ include descriptive details to support your main idea and make your answer interesting and complete?
❏ write complete sentences?
❏ fill all or most of the answer lines?
❏ check your spelling and punctuation?

Lesson 4

Identifying and Describing a Personal Experience, Part 2

Some writing questions, or **prompts**, ask you to answer an open-ended question about a reading selection. However, some prompts do not use readings. Instead, they ask you to answer a question that is based on something you know, have an opinion about, or have experienced. Generally, this type of prompt is divided into two parts.

- The first part sets the scene—it tells you what you are to write about.
- The second part tells you specifically what you are to do.

To respond to a prompt with no reading selection, apply the same 5 steps you learned in the previous lessons:

1. **READ** the prompt thoughtfully.
2. **THINK** about what the prompt asks you to write, and brainstorm ideas.
3. Organize your ideas, and then **WRITE** your answer.
4. **ASSESS** what you have written.
5. **IMPROVE** your piece of writing.

As you have learned, these steps will work for any type of open-ended question.

In this lesson, you will be asked to describe a personal experience. Plan your description by answering the six planning questions that you learned in Lesson 3:

✔ **What** is the event I will write about?
✔ **Who** was involved?
✔ **Where** did the event take place?
✔ **When** did it take place?
✔ **How** did it turn out? That is, how did the experience affect me?
✔ **Why** did it turn out the way it did?

It's important to write an answer that is interesting to read. A written response made up of sentence after sentence that begins the same way can be boring to read. You can add variety and interest to your writing by beginning sentences in different ways.

In this Lesson, you will learn how to...

- answer open-ended questions when there is no reading passage.
- vary sentences beginnings to make your writing more interesting.

READ *the question thoughtfully.*

Read the prompt carefully.

Your life has been filled with many events: starting kindergarten, entering high school, going to parties and family gatherings, celebrating birthdays and holidays, playing sports, and so on. Some events may stand out in your memory more than others.

Think about the events in your life, and choose one that stands out as especially memorable or important to you. Describe the event and explain why it is important or memorable to you.

1. What does the prompt ask you to do?

   Underline the parts of the prompt that tell you what to do. These are your key words.

   HINT: *This prompt gives more information than you need to know to answer the question. In cases like this, cross out the extra "background" information.*

   HOWEVER, be sure to read the whole prompt. The first part gives ideas about what you might choose to write about.

2. **Write the key words here.**

   _____

   _____

3. **Restate in your own words what the prompt asks you to do.**

   _____

   _____

72

STEP 2 THINK

THINK about experiences you have had that are important or memorable to you.

Begin to apply the six planning questions.

1. *What* experience are you going to write about?

   List three experiences that have made an impression on you.

   _____

   _____

   _____

HINT: *Before you chose an experience, think about*

- *how much information you remember about the experience.*
- *how easy it will be to explain the experience to someone else.*

You don't want to chose an experience that you can't write enough about to fill all the answer lines, or an experience that won't make sense "if you weren't there."

2. Select one of the experiences that you listed as the topic of your answer.

   Circle the experience you are going to use for your answer.

   Now answer the other 5 planning questions to plan your answer.

3. *Who* **was involved?**

   _____

4. *Where* **did the experience take place?**

   _____

5. **_When_ did the experience take place?**

_____

6. **_How_ did the experience turn out?**

_____

_____

7. **_Why_ did it turn out the way it did? That is, why was it important?**

_____

_____

STEP
3 **WRITE**

1. **Restate what the prompt asks you to write about.**

_____

_____

2. What is the experience you are going to write about? This is the main idea of your answer.

Write your main idea here.

_____

_____

3. **Write why this experience is important or memorable to you.**

_____

_____

_____

4. Use some key words from the prompt and your main idea to write a topic sentence.

   Write your topic sentence here.

_____

_____

_____

5. Organize your ideas. Go back to Step 2.

   Number the answers to the planning questions in the order in which you want to use them in your answer. These are your supporting details.

6. **Now write your answer.**

_____

_____

_____

_____

_____

_____

_____

HINT: *Be sure to write complete sentences.*

STEP
4   **ASSESS** *what you have written.*

How would you rate your answer based on the following rubric? Remember that the rubric assesses content, organization, word choice, sentence structure, and correct English.

4 =   I respond to the prompt clearly and accurately.
       My topic sentence repeats key words from the question.
       I state clearly why this experience is important to me.
       I include supporting details that create a picture of the experience.
       I use a variety of sentence beginnings.
       I present a well-organized answer. Planning is evident.
       I have no errors in standard English.

3 =   I respond to the prompt accurately but not completely.
       I include a topic sentence.
       My explanation of why this experience is important is not completely clear.
       I include details that for the most part explain the experience.
       I vary the ways in which some sentences begin.
       I present an organized answer.
       I have few errors in standard English, and none interfere with my meaning.

2 =   I do not answer the question completely.
       I do not have a topic sentence.
       I do not state why the experience is important to me.
       Most of the details I use do not explain the experience.
       Most of my sentences begin the same way.
       I have made numerous errors in standard English.

1 =   I do not answer the question.
       I do not have a topic sentence.
       I do not state why the experience is important to me.
       I use details that do not explain the experience.
       All my sentences begin the same way.
       I have written a disorganized answer. No planning is evident.
       I have made numerous errors in standard English.

How does your answer compare to the rubric? Before you decide, let's analyze Kenny's answer. It earned a "4."

The birth of my baby sister was an event that made a big impression on me. I am the oldest of five children—myself and four girls. When my baby sister Rhonda was born, I was ten. Jenna was nine, Mary was four, and Becky was three.

I remember that freezing December day when Rhonda was born. My mom was telling Jenna and me what to do to take care of Mary and Becky until Grandma got there. Then Mom and Dad rushed out of the house for the hospital. Jenna and I fed Mary and Becky breakfast. By then Grandma had arrived. Jenna and I grabbed our books and raced out to catch the school bus. I was excited all day. I had been hoping for a little brother ever since Mom and Dad told me another baby was coming. That school day was the longest, most boring day of my life. I could hardly wait to get home.

As soon as I got in the door, I asked Grandma if the baby had come. It had, and it was a girl. My heart sank. I threw my books on the floor. Then my grandma said to me, "That little girl is so lucky to have a big brother like you to watch over her."

Those words changed everything. It struck me like a bolt of lightning. Suddenly I realized that I was a big brother. I was ten years older than my new baby sister. When she started school, I *would be fifteen and in high school. I felt proud that I was a big*

brother. I felt responsible—mature—and I liked that feeling.

This happened right before Christmas. What a Christmas present

this was! Rhonda made me realize that as the oldest child in the

family, I would have to set the example, protect the little ones, and

help my mom and dad. Rhonda gave me a wonderful gift that

Christmas, and she didn't even know it.

What would an evaluator notice about Kenny's answer?

✔ He must have read the prompt carefully because he answered it completely and clearly.
✔ He repeats some of the key words from the prompt in his topic sentence.
✔ He states clearly why the event is important to him.
✔ He supports his answer with relevant details.
✔ He uses concrete nouns, action verbs, and vivid adjectives to make his answer interesting.
✔ He writes complete sentences.

Let's examine Kenny's answer to see why it merits a "4."

1. Kenny repeats some of the key words from the prompt in his topic sentence.

   Write his topic sentence here.

   _____

   _____

2. What is the main idea of Kenny's answer?

   Write his main idea here.

   _____

   _____

   _____

Kenny used the planning questions to organize his answer. Let's look at how he did this.

3. **_What_ is the event Kenny wrote about?**

_____

_____

4. **_Who_ is involved?**

_____

_____

5. **_Where_ does the event take place?**

_____

_____

6. **_When_ does it take place?**

_____

_____

7. **_How_ does it turn out?**

_____

_____

_____

8. **_Why_ does it turn out the way it does?**

_____

_____

_____

9. **List three descriptive details that Kenny uses to make his writing interesting.**

    _____

    _____

    _____

One reason that Kenny's answer scored so high is that it is interesting to read. Kenny uses lots of descriptive details. He also varies how he begins his sentences.

Skill: Varying Sentence Beginnings

Combining short, choppy sentences is one way to make your writing flow smoothly and interest readers. Another way is to vary the way your sentences begin. Some writers fall into the trap of starting every sentence with *I, he, she, it,* or *there.* Two ways to vary sentence beginnings are to use
- conjunctions such as *if, because, although,* and *when.*
- time, or sequence, words such as *first, second, third, next, then, finally,* and *last.*

10a. How many sentences does Kenny begin with *I?*

   Write the number here. _____

10b. How many sentences begin with other words?

   Write the number here. _____

10c. **Write a sentence from Kenny's answer that begins with a conjunction.**

   _____

   _____

   _____

When you revise your answer, look for a series of sentences that begin the same way. Rework the series so that you have a variety of sentence beginnings.

Now let's take a look at your answer.

11. Did you repeat any of the key words from the prompt in your topic sentence?

   If not, revise your topic sentence here.

   _____

   _____

   _____

12. Your topic sentence states the *what* of your personal experience. Did you forget to answer any of the other five planning questions in your response?

   Write the answers to any questions that you forgot.

   _____

   _____

   _____

   _____

   _____

   _____

   _____

13. Would adding descriptive details make your answer clearer or more interesting to the reader?

    Circle any sentences that need descriptive details.

    List some descriptive words or phrases that you could add to your answer.

    _____

    _____

    _____

    _____

    _____

14. Did you write only complete sentences?

    Underline any sentence fragments or run-on sentences, and rework them when you revise your answer.

15. Would your answer be stronger if you combined short sentences?

    Put brackets around any sentences you could combine in your revision.

STEP
5

IMPROVE *your answer.*

1. Think about the ideas you wrote when you assessed your answer.

2. Read the rubric on page 77 again. Think about your answer and about the description of a "4" paper.

3. **Use your new ideas to revise and rewrite your answer.**

_____

_____

_____

_____

_____

_____

_____

_____

_____

_____

_____

_____

_____

_____

_____

_____

_____

_____

_____

_____

_____

_____

Remember to review the "One Last Look" questions below.

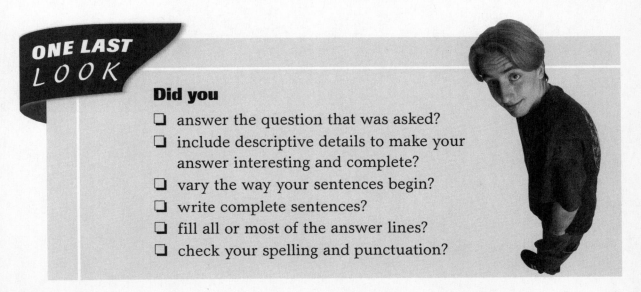

ONE LAST LOOK

Did you

❏ answer the question that was asked?

❏ include descriptive details to make your answer interesting and complete?

❏ vary the way your sentences begin?

❏ write complete sentences?

❏ fill all or most of the answer lines?

❏ check your spelling and punctuation?

Answering Questions That Ask You to Explain

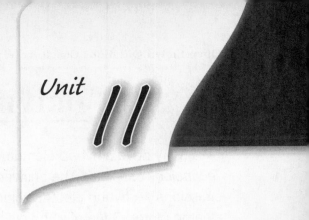

Lesson 5

Comparing and Contrasting Information

To **compare** things, you examine how they are similar. To **contrast** things, you look at how they are different. You can compare and contrast to describe, to define, or to analyze. You can also compare and contrast to show the pros and cons of an issue or the agreement and disagreement between individuals or groups.

An open-ended test question may ask you to compare and contrast
- characters in a story.
- the themes of two or more stories or poems.
- the styles of different writers.
- pros and cons of an issue.
- advantages or disadvantages of an object or idea.

In this lesson, you will focus on the advantages and disadvantages of an object. You will need to sift through a great deal of information. A T-chart is a useful tool for sorting information. By sorting information before you write, you make details easier to find as you write. Being organized in your planning helps you write an organized answer.

As you write your answer, keep working on writing complete sentences and combining short sentences. Both techniques will help improve your writing—and your test score.

In this Lesson, you will learn how to...
- answer a question that asks you to compare and contrast information by explaining advantages and disadvantages.
- use a T-chart to organize information.

DRIVING A HYBRID CAR

"Why drive a hybrid electric vehicle?" asks the U.S. Department of Energy's *Technology Snapshot.* The answer given is "(1) to improve mileage and (2) to reduce emissions." A hybrid electric vehicle (HEV) combines a small gasoline engine with an electric motor. Generally, the electric motor provides additional power for acceleration and recovers energy when the car brakes.

According to the *Technology Snapshot,* petroleum accounts for almost 95 percent of the energy used for transportation in the United States. That amounts to 8 million barrels per day just for cars and light trucks. Over half of this petroleum is imported. The amount of oil imported annually is growing as demand for oil grows.

The *Technology Snapshot* also points out that in the United States, about a third of air emissions is generated by motor vehicles. Scientists agree that burning fossil fuels for transportation generates a significant portion of the greenhouse gases that contribute to climate change. In addition to greenhouse gases, motor vehicles generate a number of other air pollutants that are considered harmful to human health and to the environment.

Let's look at how HEVs compare with conventional gasoline-powered vehicles on the two issues of fuel economy and pollution. We will limit the comparison to passenger cars. Three models of HEVs have been available for several years. For purposes of comparison and contrast, we will call them Hybrid A, Hybrid B, and Hybrid C.

The *Technology Snapshot* compares the fuel economy of the 2001 Hybrid C with two similarly equipped 2001 nonhybrid cars. We will call them Nonhybrid A and Nonhybrid B. Hybrid C gets 52 miles per gallon (mpg) in the city and 45 mpg on the highway. Nonhybrid B gets 29 mpg in the city and 33 mpg on the highway, whereas the larger Nonhybrid A gets only 23 mpg in the city and 32 mpg on the highway.

Likewise, the *Technology Snapshot* compares the fuel economies of Hybrid B and its sister nonhybrid model, which has an automatic transmission. The 2003 estimate for Hybrid B is 48 mpg in the city and 47 mpg on the highway. In contrast, the nonhybrid version gets 31 mpg in the city and 38 mpg on the highway.

Hybrid A does not have a similar gasoline-powered counterpart for use in direct comparisons. However, the *Technology Snapshot* lists the fuel economy of the 2001 model with a manual transmission: 61 mpg in the city and 68 mpg on the highway. These values are well above those of any gasoline-powered passenger car on the market. The hybrid engine is one reason for the car's fuel efficiency, but the design of the car is also a factor.

Hybrid A was designed to optimize fuel economy by combining a small engine with lightweight parts and aerodynamic features. The car's body is sleek, creating little wind resistance during driving.

The U.S. Department of Energy and the U.S. Environmental Protection Agency maintain a joint Fuel Economy Web site (www.fueleconomy.gov), where vehicles may be compared side by side. In addition to fuel economy, annual greenhouse gas emissions results are listed for each vehicle. The greenhouse gas emissions are expressed in equivalents of carbon dioxide and based on driving 15,000 miles annually. The mileage is divided so that 55 percent is considered city driving and 45 percent is considered highway driving.

Based on information on this Web site, the 2005 model of Hybrid C can be compared with similar 2005 nonhybrid models from the same carmaker. Hybrid C emits 3.5 tons of greenhouse gas, whereas Nonhybrid A and Nonhybrid B emit 6.9 tons and 5.7 tons, respectively. The 2005 Hybrid B emits 4.1 tons of greenhouse gases, whereas the conventional 5-speed manual nonhybrid emits 5.7 tons. Again, there is no model to directly compare with Hybrid A, but Hybrid A with a manual transmission emits only 3.1 tons of greenhouse gases. These results are better than those of all gasoline-powered vehicles and all other HEVs on the market.

In addition to improved gas mileage and reduced emissions, HEVs are less expensive to operate. First, because they get better fuel economy than similar gasoline-powered vehicles, they use less gasoline. This means a lower annual gasoline cost to the owner. Another saving comes in income tax. The federal government and many states offer tax incentives for driving hybrids. According to the Fuel Economy Web site, consumers who purchased a new HEV by the end of 2005 could claim a one-time federal income tax deduction of up to $2,000. They had to meet certain requirements, such as driving mostly in the United States.

Hybrid vehicles have longer warranties and longer-lasting parts than gasoline-powered vehicles. A *warranty* guarantees that parts will be replaced without charge to the owner for a certain period of time. On certain parts, Hybrid A has an 8-year/80,000-mile warranty and Hybrid C has an 8-year/100,000-mile warranty. In contrast, the typical warranty for gasoline-powered cars is 3 year/36,000 miles. The hybrid cars' longer warranties are possible because many car parts are long-lasting. The electric motor and batteries do not require maintenance during the life of the car. Brake pads on hybrids may last longer than those on conventional cars because of *regenerative braking.* This technology allows the electric motor to recover some of the energy lost during braking.

There are some disadvantages to HEVs, however. First, the cars are small. Hybrid A, for example, seats only two persons. Second, the cars do not have as much power as other vehicles because their engines are made smaller for fuel efficiency. Third, these vehicles cost more to buy than similar gasoline-powered vehicles. The technology makes them more expensive. For example, the batteries cost thousands of dollars.

Manufacturers are addressing some of these concerns by introducing more models, including light trucks and sport utility vehicles (SUVs). Many of these are comparable in size to their gasoline-powered counterparts. However, some of these larger, more powerful models of HEV are not nearly as efficient in terms of fuel consumption or emissions as Hybrid C and Hybrid A.

STEP 1

READ *the question thoughtfully.*

Read the question carefully.

"Driving a Hybrid Car" compares and contrasts hybrid cars and gasoline-powered cars. Write an essay that discusses the advantages and disadvantages of hybrids. Use relevant details from the article in your answer.

1. What does the question ask you to do?

   Underline the parts of the question that tell you what to do. These are your key words.

2. **Write the key words here.**

   _____

   _____

3. **Restate in your own words what the question asks you to do.**

   _____

   _____

HINT: *Does your restatement agree with the question? Always check your restatement against the question.*

STEP
2   **THINK**

THINK about what the article says.

1. What is the title of the article?

    Write the title here.

    _____

2. What is the main idea of the article?

    Write the main idea here.

    _____

    _____

3. What is the topic you are going to write about?

    Write the topic here.

    _____

The next step is to find details to support the comparisons and contrasts for your topic. In this case, you want to find the advantages and disadvantages of owning a hybrid car. However, if you just write these details in a single list, how will you know which are advantages and which are disadvantages? You will still have to sort the details before you begin writing. Otherwise, your answer could become a disorganized jumble of advantages and disadvantages. If you sort the details as you list them, you will save yourself time. This is the benefit of filling in a T-chart as you locate relevant details in an article or story.

Skill: Organizing Information by Using a T-Chart

A **T-chart** is a type of two-column table. It is a fast, efficient way to organize two sets of information or details—for example, advantages and disadvantages or pros and cons of an issue. (If an article or story has several points of view that you have to write about, use a multicolumn table instead.) The following diagram is a T-chart.

4a. **Label one side of the T-chart "Advantages."**

4b. **Label the other side of the T-chart "Disadvantages."**

Now fill in the T-chart.

4c. Reread the article and find the advantages and disadvantages of owning a hybrid car.

List the advantages on the chart as you locate them in the article
List the disadvantages on the chart as you locate them in the article.

HINT: *Remember that you are looking only for the advantages and disadvantages of hybrids. Ignore the information about nonhybrid cars.*

You have now gathered the details for your answer and sorted them at the same time. In planning and writing your answer, you will be able to see easily what the advantages and disadvantages are. This will help you to write a better organized answer.

HINT: *A T-chart is a graphic organizer—it organizes information visually so that relationships between pieces of information are easier to see.*

A Venn diagram is another graphic organizer that may help you with a certain type of compare-and-contrast question. If you must write about differences and similarities of two topics, sort the details in a Venn diagram. List the differences in the left and right sections. List the similarities in the center section.

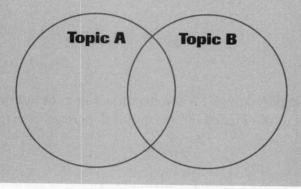

THINK about what the question asks you to do.

5. **Write the key words from Step 1 here.**

_____

_____

On your T-chart, you listed only the advantages and disadvantages. If you wrote just what was on your list, your answer would take up only a few lines. You need details to support the advantages and disadvantages.

6. **Number the advantages and disadvantages on the T-chart.**

7. Reread the article.

    On the lines below, write supporting details for the advantages of hybrids. Number each detail with the number of the advantage that it describes or explains.

    _____

    _____

    _____

    _____

    _____

8. **Now write supporting details for the disadvantages of hybrids. Number each detail with the number of the disadvantage that it describes or explains.**

    _____

    _____

    _____

    _____

STEP 3 WRITE

1. **Restate here what you are to write about.**

   _____

   _____

2. **Write your topic sentence here.**

   _____

   _____

3. Now organize your ideas. Read over the list of advantages and disadvantages that you wrote in Step 2.

   Number them in the order in which you want to use them in your answer.

You might decide to write about the advantages first, followed by the disadvantages, or the other way around. Pairing an advantage and a disadvantage is another way to organize, but this is difficult to do well. It is better to follow the organizational pattern of the article—present advantages and disadvantages separately.

4. Write your answer here.

STEP
4

ASSESS *what you have written.*

How clear, complete, and accurate is your answer? Apply the following rubric to evaluate how successfully you answered the question.

4 = I respond clearly, completely, and accurately to the question.
I include a topic sentence that repeats key words from the question.
I include all the advantages and disadvantages discussed in the article.
I include details to explain the advantages and disadvantages.
I present a well-organized answer. Planning is evident.
I have no errors in standard English.

3 = I respond to the question somewhat clearly and adequately.
I include a topic sentence.
I include all the advantages and disadvantages discussed in the article.
I present details that for the most part explain the advantages and disadvantages.
I present an organized answer.
I make some errors in standard English, but they do not interfere with my meaning.

2 = I respond to only part of the question.
I do not have a topic sentence.
I include only one advantage and one disadvantage.
I do not include details to explain the advantages and disadvantages.
I make numerous errors in standard English.

1 = I do not answer the question.
I do not have a topic sentence.
I use details as advantages and disadvantages and leave out the actual advantages and disadvantages.
My answer is disorganized. No planning is evident.
I make numerous errors in standard English.

How does your answer compare to the rubric? Before you decide, take a look at Irma's answer that earned a "4."

After reading the article, I realize that hybrid cars have both advantages and disadvantages when compared to gasoline-powered cars. There are three important advantages and three disadvantages to owning and driving hybrids.

I will discuss the advantages first. The first advantage is improved gas mileage. Second, hybrids reduce emissions. Finally, they are less expensive to operate.

The hybrid car (HEV) combines a small gasoline engine with an electric motor. Because of this combination, the amount of fuel used is reduced during acceleration and braking. For example, Hybrid C gets 52 miles per gallon (mpg) in the city and 45 mpg on the highway. In contrast, Nonhybrid B gets 23 mpg in the city and 32 mpg on the highway. The hybrid gets much better gas mileage.

Protecting our environment is important. One way to protect the environment is to improve our air quality. Driving a hybrid car can help us do just that. The hybrid car reduces gas emissions, which in turn reduces the greenhouse effect on our climate.

In addition to these two advantages, the hybrid car is less expensive to operate. Because of good gas mileage, less money is spent on gasoline. Also, many state governments and the federal government offer tax incentives for driving a hybrid car. Hybrids offer longer warranties, so more parts are covered for a longer time. The car owner does not have to pay for parts under warranty. The electric motor and batteries do not require any maintenance during the life of the car. The brakes last longer on hybrids, too.

On the other hand, not everything about a hybrid car is an advantage. The disadvantages are the size, the lack of power, and the cost of the car. First, the HEV is generally smaller in size than a gasoline-powered car. One HEV model seats only two people. Second, the combination electric motor and gasoline-powered engine results in a less powerful car than the gasoline-powered engine. Finally, the car is more expensive to buy than a similar gasoline-powered car. The technology that runs the HEV is expensive.

These are the advantages and disadvantages of driving and owning a hybrid car. If I were buying, I would buy a hybrid because I care about the environment.

What would an evaluator think about Irma's answer?
- ✔ She must have read the question carefully, because she answers it completely, clearly, and accurately.
- ✔ She repeats key words from the question in her topic sentence.
- ✔ She includes all 3 advantages and all 3 disadvantages of hybrid cars.
- ✔ She supports her answer with important details from the article.
- ✔ She writes complete sentences.
- ✔ She fills all the answer lines.

Let's examine Irma's answer to see why it merits a "4."

1. Irma repeats some of the key words from the question in her topic sentence.

   Write her topic sentence here.

   _____

   _____

2. She includes all 3 advantages in her answer.

   Write the 3 advantages here.

   _____

   _____

   _____

3. Irma includes the 3 disadvantages.

   Write those 3 disadvantages here.

   _____

   _____

   _____

4. Irma uses transitions to help the reader spot information in her answer. She uses *first, second,* and *third* to identify the advantages. What transitions does she use to signal the disadvantages?

   Write those transition words here.

   _____

Irma uses details from the article to explain the advantages and disadvantages.

5. **Write one of the details that she uses to explain an advantage.**

   _____

   _____

6. **Write one of the details that she uses to explain a disadvantage.**

_____

_____

Now let's take a look at your answer.

7. Did you repeat part of the question in your topic sentence?

   If not, revise your topic sentence here.

_____

_____

_____

8. Did you include all 3 advantages and all 3 disadvantages in your answer?

   Circle Yes or No.

9. If you circled "No," what did you forget? Go back to your T-chart in Step 2 and review your information.

   Write the advantages or disadvantages that you forgot to include in your answer.

_____

_____

_____

_____

10. Did you use details in your answer to explain the advantages and disadvantages?

    Circle Yes or No.

11. If you circled "No," what details could you add? Review your T-chart.

Write additional details here.

_____

_____

_____

_____

12. Did you write complete sentences? Check for fragments or run-on sentences in your answer.

Underline any fragments or run-ons.

Correct those sentences here.

_____

_____

_____

_____

_____

_____

13. Would your answer read more smoothly if you combined some sentences?

Put brackets around sentences that you could combine in your revision.

STEP 5

IMPROVE *your answer.*

1. Think about the ideas you wrote when you assessed your answer.

2. Read the rubric on page 99 again. Think about your answer and about the description of a "4" paper.

3. **Use your new ideas to revise and rewrite your answer.**

_____

_____

_____

_____

_____

_____

_____

_____

_____

_____

_____

_____

_____

_____

_____

_____

_____

_____

_____

_____

_____

_____

_____

_____

_____

_____

_____

_____

Remember to review the "One Last Look" questions below.

ONE LAST LOOK

Did you
- ❑ answer the question that was asked?
- ❑ include the three advantages and the three disadvantages?
- ❑ include details to explain the advantages and disadvantages completely?
- ❑ write complete sentences?
- ❑ fill all or most of the answer lines?
- ❑ check your spelling and punctuation?

Lesson 6

Explaining Cause and Effect

When explaining a cause-and-effect relationship, you are explaining why something happens—the **cause**—and what happens as a result—the **effect**.

There are different kinds of cause-and-effect relationships.

- A single effect may result from a number of causes.
  - → The pitcher was sluggish (effect) because he had not pitched for four days (cause) and the game had been interrupted twice for rain delays (cause).

- A single cause may result in a number of effects.
  - → The rain delays (cause) caused the pitcher to lose his momentum (effect) and to pitch inconsistently (effect).

- There may be a chain reaction of causes and effects.
  - → The rain delays (cause) caused the pitcher to lose momentum (effect/cause), which allowed the opposing team to hit two runs (effect/cause) and forced the manager to pull the pitcher from the game (effect).

To answer a cause-and-effect question, you must

  ✔ distinguish between the cause(s) and effect(s).
  - To identify a cause ask, "Why did this happen?"
  - To identify an effect ask, "What happened because of this?"
  ✔ state clearly in your topic sentence what you are discussing: causes, effects, or both.
  ✔ organize your supporting details clearly in either
  - **chronological order:** the order in which the causes and effects occurred. OR
  - **order of importance:** an arrangement of causes and their effects from least important to most important, or vice versa.

Using transition words that show cause-and-effect relationships will help your ideas flow smoothly from one to the next. This will help your readers understand what you are trying to say.

In this Lesson, you will learn how to...

- answer a question that asks you to explain cause and effect.
- use a concept map to organize information.
- use transitions to highlight cause-and-effect relationships.

WHAT WOULD WE DO WITHOUT RADIO WAVES?

Imagine that you don't have a microwave; how would you make popcorn? Or imagine how you'd get along without your cell phone; how would you contact your friends? And what about finding directions to the movies? Some people use their GPS (Global Positioning System) to figure it out.

What do these three technologies have in common? They are all relatively recent technological developments based on radio waves. Each has introduced convenience into our fast-paced lives—and added to the fast pace.

Microwave ovens use radio waves with a frequency of about 2.5 gigahertz, called *microwaves,* to heat polar molecules in food. This method is much faster than conventional heating by conduction, used by the regular oven. With microwaves, only the food heats up. The air, the microwave oven, and containers made of glass, plastic, or paper do not. As a result, microwaving is a fast and energy-efficient method of cooking.

Microwave cooking was discovered by accident by Percy Spencer in 1945. He noticed that a candy bar melted in his pocket when he was standing next to a magnetron, a device that generates microwaves. The magnetron was initially used for radar. The first microwave oven was not developed until 1947. It was as big as a refrigerator and cost between $2,000 and $3,000. It was hardly suitable for home use. In 1967, a countertop model costing around $500 came on the market. In the 1970s and 1980s, microwave cooking became very popular. According to The Great Idea Finder Web site, "Today, Percy Spencer's radar boxes melt chocolate and pop popcorn in millions of homes around the world," including over 90% of U.S. homes.

Microwave ovens became popular quickly because they met the desire for convenience at a time when changes in society were increasing the pace of life. Women were entering the workforce in greater numbers. Many households had two wage-earners—mother and father. More families were headed by a single parent. In addition, parents and children were becoming involved in more and more activities outside the home. Families found that they had more money than time for cooking and eating. To meet the needs of consumers, food marketers began to offer more frozen food choices and ready-made items that needed only to be heated in order to put a meal on the table.

Homes were not the only place where microwave ovens were used. They turned up in cafeterias, grocery stores, convenience stores, workplace lunchrooms, and food marts at gasoline stations. A quick meal or snack could be warmed and ready to go in minutes or seconds. The eating patterns of Americans have changed over the past 50 years, and microwave ovens have contributed greatly to these changes.

Cell phones are a modern combination of two older technologies, the radio and the telephone. Cell phones are essentially very sophisticated radios. Today, there are several cell phone access technologies. Each uses different radio wave frequencies. In the United States, cell phones typically operate between 824 and 894 megahertz, although some operate at 1900 megahertz (1.9 gigahertz). The international standard that is used in most of the rest of the world is called GSM (Global System for Mobile communications). This digital technology operates in two bands, at 900 megahertz and at 1800 megahertz. The GSM standard was established in Europe in the 1980s, which was well before digital cell phones were introduced in the United States. In the United States, the analog standard AMPS (Advanced Mobile Phone System) was the first system for cell phones. It was introduced in Chicago in 1983.

Cell phones give us the convenience of being able to talk to anyone, anywhere at anytime. No longer do people have to be at home or in the office to make or receive phone calls. This mobility has given us great freedom. Many people justified their first cell phone purchase for emergency use. That idea has been replaced by the convenience that cell phones afford us. Today's cell phones are loaded with features including calendar functions, video-conferencing, e-mail, cameras, and games. They can be used as much for entertainment as for communication.

About 90% of people living in Europe and Asia own cell phones, which is a higher rate than in the United States. A few years ago an estimated 20% of teenagers in the United States owned a cell phone. That number is increasing daily.

The Global Positioning System (GPS) is actually a collection of satellites orbiting Earth. This network was developed by the U.S. military as a navigation system, but it is now available to the public. The system operates on radio wave frequencies between 1.2 and 1.6 gigahertz. A GPS receiver detects radio transmissions from four or more satellites. It then determines its distance from each, and combines this information with an electronic almanac to determine its own location—anywhere on Earth!

Some vehicles now come with GPS receivers as standard equipment, but hand-held devices are available for under $100. These devices display position on a map; track route of travel; and calculate distance, the time traveled, the speed, and the estimated time of arrival. This technology is not yet as widespread as cell phones or microwave ovens, but consider the possibility of being able to travel anywhere without getting lost. Just like cell phones and microwave ovens, GPS devices will become standard equipment. Someday, no one will remember when people had to use paper maps to figure out the route from one place to another.

Radio waves—we can't see them, hear them, or feel them, but we use them every day in a multitude of devices that make our lives easier. Microwave ovens, cell phones, and GPS systems are just a few examples. Other examples include garage door openers (40 megahertz), baby monitors (49 megahertz), cordless phones (900 megahertz), and air traffic control radar (960 to 1200 megahertz).

READ *the question thoughtfully.*

Read the question carefully.

The article states, "Radio waves—we can't see them, hear them, or feel them, but we use them every day in a multitude of devices that make our lives easier." Explain how three technologies using radio waves have made our lives easier. Use relevant information from the article in your explanation.

HINT: *Note the word* relevant *in the question. It means that the information you use in your answer must be related to your main idea. Instead of using just any facts from the article, you must choose details that fit the point you want to make in your answer.*

1. What does the question ask you to do?

   Underline the parts of the question that tell you what to do. These are your key words.

2. **Write those key words here.**

   _____

   _____

3. **Restate in your own words what the question asks you to do.**

   _____

   _____

HINT: *Always check your restatement against the question before you continue.*

STEP
2   **THINK**

THINK about what the article says.

1. What is the title of the article?

   Write the title here.

   _____

2. What is the main idea of the article?

   Write the main idea here.

   _____

   _____

3. The article describes three technological developments that have resulted from the use of radio waves.

   List the three technological developments here.

   _____

4. Are these three technologies causes or effects, or both?

   Write your answer here. _____

If you wrote "both," you are correct. Each is an *effect* of new ways of using radio waves, and each is a *cause* of how our lives have changed. The question asks you to explain how each technology is a cause—that is, how each has made our lives easier.

5. What are the causes that you are going to write about?

   Write the causes here, and number them 1, 2, and 3.

   _____

   _____

   _____

6. Go back to the article.

   Number each paragraph that describes a cause, using the numeral 1, 2, or 3 to match the cause listed in number 5.

THINK about what the question asks you to do.

7. **Write the key words from the question that you identified in Step 1.**

   _____

   _____

HINT: *To write a well-developed answer, you should use at least three details to explain each cause. But just any three details won't work. Select only details that help you answer the question. The question asks you to describe how these three technologies have made our lives easier. Therefore, you do not need to include the bandwidth for cell phones. That detail is not relevant. Neither is the fact that the military developed GPS.*

Before you can decide which details to include, you need to locate them in the article. As you locate details, organize the ones you might want to use. If you organize details as you locate them, it will be easier to use them as you write.

Skill: Organizing Information by Using a Concept Map

Using a **concept map** is a good method for organizing information. A concept map is also called a **concept web.** It is a visual way to show information that you might use in your answer.

8a. **Label each circle on pages 116–117 with one of the causes you are writing about.**

8b. Look back at number 6 to see which paragraphs in the article describe each cause. For each cause, choose relevant details that you could use in your answer. Don't stop at three details if you find more than three relevant details. At this step in planning your writing, you want to know *all* the relevant information that you could use to answer the question.

Draw lines out from each circle, like spokes on a wheel. Write one detail about that cause on each line.

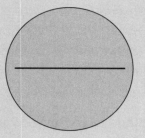

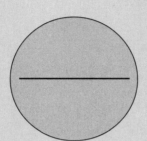

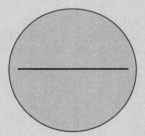

The concept map makes it easy for you to see the information you have for each cause. This will make writing your answer easier. You won't have to read through the article each time you need to add a detail.

STEP
3 **WRITE**

1. **Write the main idea of your answer.**

   _____

   _____

2. Combine the main idea with some key words from the question to create a topic sentence.

   Write your topic sentence here.

   _____

   _____

   _____

3. Now go back to Step 2 and review your concept map. Which details do you want to use to explain each cause?

   Number the details you want to use in the order in which you want to use them.

4. **Now write your answer.**

   _____

   _____

   _____

   _____

   _____

   _____

STEP 4

ASSESS *what you have written.*

What do you think a teacher-evaluator would say about your answer? Apply the rubric and see how your answer measures up.

4 = I answer the question clearly, completely, and accurately.
I include a topic sentence that includes some key words from the question.
I state the three causes clearly and accurately.
I develop each cause with relevant details.
I use cause-and-effect transition words.
I use complete and correct sentences.

3 = I answer the question accurately but not completely.
I include a topic sentence.
I state the three causes accurately.
I state details that for the most part are relevant to the causes.
I use a few cause-and-effect transition words.
I use complete and correct sentences.

2 = I answer the question, but not clearly and completely.
I do not have a topic sentence.
I state the causes, but not clearly.
Most of the details I use are not relevant, making my explanation unclear.
I do not use cause-and-effect transition words.
I do not use complete and correct sentences.

1 = I do not answer the question.
I do not include a topic sentence.
I do not state the causes accurately or use relevant details to develop them.
My writing is choppy and difficult to understand.
I do not use cause-and-effect transition words.
I do not use complete and correct sentences.

How does your answer measure up to the rubric? Before you decide, let's analyze Philip's paper. It earned a "4."

Recent technologies based on the use of radio waves have made our lives easier. Three of these technologies have become an essential part of our everyday life. They are the microwave, the cell phone, and the Global Positioning System (GPS).

The microwave can be found in 90 percent of U.S. homes. Because the microwave is a convenient and fast way to prepare a meal and because we are so busy, many people use it. In many families, both parents work or there is a single parent. It is fast and simple to cook or reheat food in a microwave and have dinner on the table in a few minutes. Microwaves are also used in restaurants, cafeterias, workplace lunchrooms, convenience stores, and food marts at gas stations. It makes eating on the run easy.

The cell phone is another technology based on radio waves. In the beginning, many people had cell phones for emergency use only. This is no longer true. Cell phones let us stay connected to people in our lives at all times. Consequently, today's cell phone makes life easier. It has a calendar, camera, e-mail, and games. As a result, it is more than a phone. It is an entertainment center.

The Global Positioning System is another technology based on radio waves. This system displays maps, can track a travel route, calculate distance, and estimate arrival time. Because of all these *functions, GPS receivers are standard equipment on some cars. Handheld GPS systems are available for under $100. With a GPS system you can travel anywhere without getting lost.*

Radio waves have certainly resulted in devices that make our life easier. I know my family could not live without our microwave or cell phones. We do not have GPS yet. After reading this article, I wonder how can we do without one!

What do you think an evaluator would say about Philip's answer?

- ✔ He must have read the question carefully because he answered it completely, clearly, and accurately.
- ✔ He repeats some of the key words from the question in his topic sentence.
- ✔ He states the causes clearly and develops each cause with relevant details.
- ✔ He uses cause-and-effect transition words.
- ✔ He writes complete sentences.

Let's examine Philip's answer to see why it merits a "4."

1. Philip repeats some of the key words from the question in his topic sentence.

   Write Philip's topic sentence here.

   _____

   _____

2. Philip names three technologies that use radio waves.

   List those three technologies here.

   _____

   _____

   _____

3. How many paragraphs does Philip write?

   Write the number here. _____

4. How many of these paragraphs does he use to explain the three technologies?

   Write the number here. _____

5. Philip explains each technology, or cause of easier lives, using details.

   Write one sentence that he uses to explain each technology.

   Technology 1: _____

   _____

   Technology 2: _____

   _____

   Technology 3: _____

   _____

Philip's answer is clear and reads smoothly because he uses transitions to move from one idea to the next.

Skill: Using Cause-and-Effect Transition Words

A **transition** is a word that connects ideas or sentences. **Cause-and-effect transition words** make connections for the reader between what happened and why it happened. Using cause-and-effect transitions will help your reader understand the relationships between causes and effects.

Cause-and-Effect Words

as a consequence	because	if . . . then
consequently	because of	so
as a result	due to	so that
therefore		

6. Find the transitions that Philip uses in his answer.

   Write the transitions here.

   Paragraph 2: _____

   Paragraph 3: _____

   Paragraph 4: _____

Did you use any cause-and-effect transition words in your answer? Think about adding some when you revise your answer.

Now let's take a look at your answer.

7. Did you repeat any of the key words in your topic sentence?

   If not, revise your topic sentence here.

   _____

   _____

   _____

8. How many relevant details did you use to describe the microwave?

   Write the number here. _____

9. Reread your answer. Did you use any details that are not relevant to your idea about microwaves? (Look for details that could be dropped without making your answer less complete, clear, and accurate.)

   Circle Yes or No.

   If you circled "Yes," cross out the irrelevant details about the microwave in your answer.

10. Would adding more relevant details about microwaves help to develop your answer more completely and clearly?

    Circle Yes or No.

    If you circled "Yes," write additional details here.

    _____

    _____

    _____

    _____

    _____

Now go through the same process to review the details you used to explain cell phones and GPS.

11. Review your section on cell phones. Do you need to cross out irrelevant information?

    Circle Yes or No.

    If you circled "Yes," cross out the irrelevant details about cell phones in your answer.

12. Do you need to add relevant details about cell phones?

    Circle Yes or No.

    If you circled "Yes," write additional details about cell phones here.

    _____

    _____

    _____

    _____

    _____

13. Review your section on GPS. Did you use any irrelevant details?

    Circle Yes or No.

    If you circled "Yes," cross out the irrelevant details about GPS in your answer.

14. Would adding more relevant details about GPS make your answer more complete and clearer?

    If you circled "Yes," write additional details here.

    _____

    _____

    _____

    _____

    _____

15. Have you used cause-and-effect words? If not, would using some make your answer clearer and easier to understand?

    If adding some would make your answer stronger, circle places in your answer where you could add cause-and-effect words in the revision step.

16. Does your answer have any sentence fragments or run-on sentences?

    Put brackets around any incomplete sentences or run-on sentences. Correct them in your revision.

STEP 5

IMPROVE *your answer.*

1. Think about the ideas you wrote when you assessed your answer.

2. Read the rubric on page 120 again. Think about your answer and about the description of a "4" paper.

3. **Use your new ideas to revise and rewrite your answer.**

_____

_____

_____

_____

_____

_____

_____

_____

_____

_____

_____

_____

_____

_____

_____

_____

_____

_____

_____

_____

_____

_____

_____

_____

_____

_____

_____

Remember to review the "One Last Look" questions below.

ONE LAST LOOK

Did you

- ❏ answer the question that was asked?
- ❏ include relevant details to make your answer interesting, accurate, and complete?
- ❏ write complete sentences?
- ❏ fill all or most of the answer lines?
- ❏ check your spelling and punctuation?

Lesson 7

Explaining Steps in a Process

A test question may ask you to explain how to do something, or to describe how something works. This type of question is asking you to explain **steps in a process**. The process may be how to make something, how to play a game, how to get from here to there, or how to achieve a goal. Your first reaction may be to start with step 1, move to step 2, then on to step 3, and so on. You would be writing a list of what to do, or of how something works. However, a list in sentence form will not earn a great score. You must present the steps in the process in an interesting manner.

When you are asked to explain a process, you must
- identify what the process is as your main idea.
- select only details that will make the steps clear, complete, and accurate.
- organize the details in the order they should be done.
- use sequence words to help the reader move from one step to the next.

To catch the reader's interest, you must present the information in an interesting way. Your choice of details and how you express them will help you with this strategy. However, your answer also has to be clear and easy to follow. Using transition words that show **sequence**, or order, will help you to do this.

In this Lesson, you will learn how to...
- answer a question that asks you to explain a process.
- use sequence words to make the steps easy to follow.

ON THE ROAD TO A DRIVER'S LICENSE

"Good afternoon, students," the principal said to the sophomores assembled in the auditorium. "Today's assembly is to inform you of the steps you must take to get your driver's license. The school plays a part in this because, as some of you know, you must take a required driver's education class this year. Josh Brown, from the motor-vehicle department, will speak to you today to explain the process. Please give Mr. Brown your undivided attention."

"Thank you, Principal Novack. Hello, everyone. I'm going to walk you through the process of getting your license. There are many steps," said Mr. Brown. "Before you even get behind the wheel of a car for the first time, you must do a lot of work to prepare yourself. Here's how the process works.

"You start with the driver's education class in your sophomore year. You don't get to drive a car in that class. You just learn the basic rules of driving, such as what to do at a four-way stop. You learn what the different street signs mean and about how important it is to wear a seatbelt and obey the speed limit. You are quizzed every Friday on what you learned in class during the week. This information may seem boring, but it's really important. It prepares you for the written test you must pass to get your license. More important, you must understand the rules of the road to be a good and safe driver.

"At the end of the semester, you must pass a written examination. You cannot move on to the next step in the process if you do not pass the exam. If you get a B or higher in the class, you can save money on your insurance when you do get your license.

"After you complete and pass the sophomore-year driver's ed class, you need to take eight hours of driver's education in an actual car. A few high schools in the state offer this class to students during school time, but Mr. Novack tells me that your school does not. An adult such as a parent may provide this instruction, but I suggest that you sign up to take classes at a private driving school. You can choose the driving school you would like to use. There are 10 driving schools in our county. You should contact at least 5 schools to inquire about their fees. You should also speak to some people who have used each before you decide which school to sign up with.

"Once you decide on a driving school, call the school to schedule your driving lessons. You will not have to pay the school until after you complete your eight one-hour lessons. The week before your first driving lesson, you should review the book you were given in your sophomore driver's ed class and your class notes. This will help you mentally prepare for your first lesson.

"For your first lesson, the driving instructor will meet you at your house. You will get behind the wheel immediately. The instructor will sit in the passenger seat and guide you. Don't worry about messing up. Driver-instruction cars are specially designed with a steering wheel and gas and break pedals for both the driver's and passenger's seats. The driving instructor can take over at any time. Once the instructor touches his or her steering wheel, gas pedal, or break pedal, your controls are disabled.

"For your first three lessons, you will drive on residential and local streets. Then, for the next two lessons, the instructor will teach you how to drive on the highway. Your final three lessons will be a combination of driving on highways and local streets and learning to park the car.

"After you successfully complete your eight hours of driving lessons, you will receive your learner's permit. In this state, you will have your learner's permit for one year before you can apply for your driver's license. Your learner's permit allows you to drive with a licensed driver over the age of 18 during daylight hours for the first six months. For the remaining six months of your learner's permit, you are allowed to drive at night with a licensed driver over the age of 18.

"The last steps occur when your one-year learner's permit is drawing to a close. That's when you need to contact your driving school again. The driving school will schedule an appointment with the motor-vehicle department for you to take your road test. An instructor will pick you up on the day of your road test and drive you to the motor-vehicle department.

"Before the day of your road test, it is a good idea to review your information booklet from sophomore year again. When you get to the motor-vehicle department, you will first have to take a written test. The written test is taken on a computer, so you will receive your score immediately. If you pass, you are ready for the road test. You will get behind the wheel of the test car. A motor-vehicle employee will sit in the passenger seat and grade you on your performance. You will first drive around a track to a stop sign. Make sure you stop completely. Next, you will have to parallel park. Your final test will be to execute a four-point turn. You will then return to the motor-vehicle department.

"If you are given a passing grade on the road test, you will get in line to get your license. An employee will take your picture and attach it to a form with your name, address, and signature on it. You will wait approximately 10 minutes for your license to be created and laminated. When your license is ready, your name will be called and you will be given your license. The driving school instructor will take you home, and you'll be ready to go!"

STEP
1

READ *the question thoughtfully.*

Read the question carefully.

 After the assembly, Principal Novack asked the students to inform a parent or guardian of the steps to be taken to get a driver's license. Using information from the passage, write a letter explaining the process of getting a driver's license.

1. What does the question ask you to do?

    Underline the parts of the question that tell you what to do. These are your key words.

2. **Write those key words here.**

    _____

    _____

3. **Restate in your own words what the question asks you to do.**

    _____

    _____

HINT: *How do you know if your restatement matches the question? Check your restatement against the question to be sure.*

THINK about what the story says.

1. What is the title of the story?

   Write the title here.

   _____

2. How many basic steps are there in getting a driver's license?

   Count the number of basic steps and write the number here. _____

   > **HINT:** *Locate and remember the steps by numbering them in the margin. But don't confuse descriptive details with the basic actions of getting a driver's license. The author includes descriptive details to help the reader understand what will happen in each step, but these details are not steps.*

3. **List the basic steps here.**

   _____

   _____

   _____

   _____

   _____

   _____

   _____

4. **List details to explain each step. As you list each detail, number it (1, 2, 3, etc.) to match the step in number 3 that it explains.**

_____

_____

_____

_____

_____

_____

_____

_____

_____

_____

_____

_____

_____

_____

THINK about what the question asks you to do.

5. **Write the key words from the question again.**

_____

_____

STEP 3 WRITE

1. What is the main idea of your answer?

   Write the main idea here.

   _____

   _____

2. You need a topic sentence that states the main idea of your letter.

   Write your topic sentence here.

   _____

   _____

   _____

HINT: *Remember to begin your letter with*
    Dear _____ **,**
and to end it with
    Sincerely yours,
    [your name]

3. Organize your ideas. Review the key words and the details you wrote in Step 2. **Place a check mark next to the details you want to use in your answer.**

4. **Now write your answer.**

_____

_____

_____

_____

_____

_____

_____

_____

_____

_____

_____

_____

_____

_____

_____

_____

_____

_____

_____

_____

HINT: *How long should your answer be? How many lines does the answer sheet have? That's how long your answer should be.*

STEP
4

ASSESS *what you have written.*

The following rubric is similar to ones that teachers use to evaluate student writing. How do you think your answer measures up to the rubric for organization, content, sentence structure, word choice, and standard English grammar and usage?

4 = I respond clearly, completely, and accurately to the question.
I state the main idea in the topic sentence.
I include all steps in a logical order.
I include descriptive details to make each step clear and interesting.
I use sequence words to move from one step to the next.
I use complete, correct sentences.

3 = I respond to the question accurately and completely, but not clearly.
I state the main idea in the topic sentence.
I include most of the steps, in the correct order.
I include some details that describe the steps.
I use a few sequence words to move from one step to the next.
I use complete, correct sentences.

2 = I do not answer the question completely.
I state the main idea, but not clearly.
I include some of the steps, but the order is not correct.
I include a few supporting details and some unnecessary details.
I use almost no sequence words.
I make some errors in standard English.

1 = I do not answer the question.
I do not have a topic sentence.
I include a few steps, but they are not in the correct order.
I include irrelevant details.
I use no sequence words.
I make numerous errors in standard English.

How does your answer compare to the rubric? Before you decide, take a look at Sara's answer that earned a "2."

Dear Dad,

Yes, it is here. I am eligible to get a driver's license. I know that means your automobile insurance will increase. I have listened carefully to what I need to do to get my license. I will follow the steps exactly, I will become a superior driver who qualifies for a good driver insurance discount.

The principal asked us to write a letter explaining how to get a driver's license. Well, here it is.

I must take the driver's ed class at school this year. I take behind-the-wheel driving for eight hours. Then I get my learner's permit. After one year, I can get my license after taking a written test and a driving test. I can hardly wait.

Sincerely,

Sara

What would an evaluator say about Sara's answer?

✔ She read the question but does not answer it completely.

✔ She does not state the main idea of her letter.

✔ She includes most of the steps, and the order is correct.

✔ She lists the steps without including details to develop the ideas.

✔ She includes details that are not relevant. Her answer is disorganized.

✔ She uses only two sequence words.

✔ She has a run-on sentence.

Let's examine Sara's answer to see why it merits a "2." What could Sara do to improve her answer?

1. What is Sara's topic sentence? You will have to look hard for it because Sara placed it after several sentences of unnecessary details.

    Write her topic sentence here.

    _____

    _____

2. Sara includes most of the steps. Which step is Sara's answer missing?

    Write the step that she left out.

    _____

    _____

3. Sara includes irrelevant details that make her answer disorganized.

    Write those unnecessary details here.

    _____

    _____

    _____

    _____

    _____

4. What details should Sara use instead?

   Write three relevant details here that Sara does not use in her answer.

   _____

   _____

   _____

5. Sara has written a run-on sentence.

   Correct her run-on sentence here.

   _____

   _____

Sara uses two sequence words in her answer. Sequence words let readers know when the writer is moving from one idea or step to the next.

Skill: Using Sequence Words

A **sequence word** is a transition that signals the order in which something is done. It also shows when one step or idea ends and the next one begins. Using sequence words makes it easier for the reader to understand steps in a process.

Read these driving directions, which do not use sequence words:

> You get to the store by driving south on Highway 101. Highway 92 east. Metro Center Boulevard. Exit. Turn left.

Now read these directions that use sequence words:

> You get to the store by first driving south on Highway 101 until you reach Highway 92. Then take Highway 92 east for a short while. Next, exit at the Metro Center Blvd. At the traffic light at the bottom of the hill, turn left. Go 1 mile. Finally, you will see the store on the right.

Which set of directions is easier to follow? A piece of writing, especially one that discusses steps in a process, is like a set of driving directions. Without sequence words, it makes little sense. With sequence words, the ideas are easy to follow and understand.

Sequence Words

first, second, third	before	then, next, subsequently
one, two, three	finally, last, later	now, soon, until
after, afterwards	following this	

6. Which two sequence words does Sara use in her answer?

   Write the two sequence words here.

   _____

Did you include any sequence words in your answer? Think about adding some when you revise your answer.

Now let's take a look at your answer.

7. Did you use any of the key words from the question in your topic sentence?

   If not, revise your topic sentence here.

   _____

   _____

   _____

> **HINT: *The reason to use key words from the question in your topic sentence is to remind you what you are supposed to write about.***

8. Did you include all the steps in getting a driver's license as explained in the passage?

   Circle Yes or No.

9. If you circled "No," reread the passage to find the steps you missed.

   Write the missing steps here.

   _____

   _____

   _____

   _____

10. Did you explain the steps in the correct order?

    Circle Yes or No.

11. **If you circled "No," number the steps in your answer in the correct order.**

12. Did you include details to develop each step? If not, what details could you include?

    Write additional details here.

    _____

    _____

    _____

    _____

    _____

    _____

13. Would your answer be easier to understand if you added sequence words to show when one step ends and another begins?

    If so, circle places in your answer where you could add sequence words.

14. Did you write any sentence fragments or run-on sentences in your answer?

    Put brackets around any sentence fragments or run-on sentences. Rework these sentences when you revise your answer.

IMPROVE *your answer.*

1. Think about your suggestions to improve Sara's answer.

2. Think about the ideas you wrote when you assessed your answer.

3. Read the rubric on page 139 again. Think about your answer and about the description of a "4" paper.

4. **Use your new ideas to revise and rewrite your answer.**

_____

_____

_____

_____

_____

_____

_____

_____

_____

_____

_____

_____

_____

_____

_____

_____

_____

_____

_____

_____

Remember to review the "One Last Look" questions below.

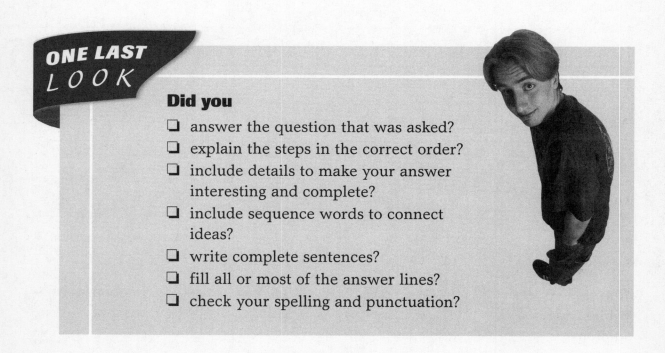

ONE LAST *LOOK*

Did you

- ❏ answer the question that was asked?
- ❏ explain the steps in the correct order?
- ❏ include details to make your answer interesting and complete?
- ❏ include sequence words to connect ideas?
- ❏ write complete sentences?
- ❏ fill all or most of the answer lines?
- ❏ check your spelling and punctuation?

Answering Questions That Ask You to Analyze

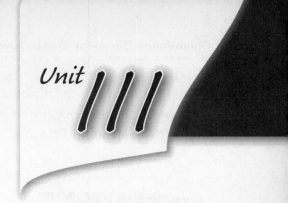

Lesson 8

Expressing Your Opinion

How did you like the last movie you saw? What's your favorite TV show? What do you think about the home team's chances of winning the playoffs? Who are you voting for in the election? Why?

Your answers to these questions are opinions. An **opinion** is your point of view, based primarily on personal judgment. You form your opinion based on your experience. Your experience is all that has happened to you in life and all you have done. It also includes all that you have read, heard, and seen in movies and on TV.

On a test, you may find an open-ended question that asks you to give your opinion about a subject. Often, these questions are based on literary topics. You might find a question that asks

- what you think the author's message is in a passage.
- why you think the author chose the particular title for a passage.
- whether the use of imagery helps or hinders your understanding of a poem.
- why you think a character reacts as he or she does in a story.
- whether you agree or disagree with an argument, and why.

When you are asked to give your opinion about a subject, you must explain
  ✔ what you think about the subject.
  ✔ why you think that way; that is, the reasons for your opinion.

The reasons are the facts that support your opinion. A **fact**
- is generally accepted as true.
- can be proved true.
- can be checked for accuracy.

Your opinion should be based on facts. If you are giving your opinion about a work of literature, use examples from the work as your "facts"—reasons to support your opinion.

Transition words are important signals for your reader whether you are giving your own opinion or someone else's. In this lesson, you will practice using words that indicate the addition of information.

In this Lesson, you will learn how to...

- answer a question that asks for your opinion.
- use transition words to signal the addition of information.

I HEAR AMERICA SINGING

by Walt Whitman

I hear America singing, the varied carols I hear,

Those of mechanics, each one singing his as it should be blithe* and strong,

The carpenter singing his as he measures his plank or beam,

The mason singing his as he makes ready for work, or leaves off work,

The boatman singing what belongs to him in his boat, the deckhand singing on the steamboat deck,

The shoemaker singing as he sits on his bench, the hatter singing as he stands,

The wood-cutter's song, the ploughboy's on his way in the morning, or at the noon intermission or at sundown,

The delicious singing of the mother, or of the young wife at work, or of the girl sewing or washing,

Each singing what belongs to him or her and to none else,

The day what belongs to the day—at night, the party of young fellows, robust, friendly,

Singing with open mouths their strong melodious songs.

blithe: cheerful

STEP 1

READ *the question thoughtfully.*

Read the question carefully.

> **After reading "I Hear America Singing," how do you think Walt Whitman sees America? Use words and details from the poem to support your opinion.**

1. What does the question ask you to do?

    Underline the parts of the question that tell you what to do. These are your key words.

2. **Write those key words here.**

    _____

    _____

3. **Restate in your own words what the question asks you to do.**

    _____

    _____

HINT: *How do you know if your restatement is accurate? Always check it against the question to be sure.*

STEP 2 THINK

THINK about what the poem says.

1. What is the title of the poem?

   Write the title here.

   _____

2. **Write the first line of the poem here.**

   _____

3. What does this line mean to you?

   Write your opinion here.

   _____

   _____

   _____

   _____

4. Whitman wrote what is often called a list poem. He states the details almost as though he were listing things.

Write Whitman's list of people here.

_____

_____

_____

_____

_____

_____

_____

_____

_____

_____

5. Go back to number 4.

Next to each person, write the detail that Whitman gives for that person.

6. Why do you think the poet listed all these people?

   Write your opinion here.

   _____

   _____

   _____

   _____

7. **Write the last line of the poem here.**

   _____

8. What does this line mean to you?

   Write your opinion here.

   _____

   _____

   _____

   _____

THINK about what the question asks you to do.

9. **Write the key words here that you wrote in Step 1.**

   _____

   _____

10. Now think about what the poem says and about what the question asks. How do you think Whitman sees America?

Write your opinion here. This is your main idea for your answer.

_____

_____

_____

11. Review the details from number 5, above. What ideas of your own does this list create in your mind? What details could you add to these people and descriptions to support your opinion?

Write additional details that you can think of to support your opinion.

_____

_____

_____

_____

_____

STEP 3 **WRITE**

1. **Write your main idea/opinion again.**

_____

_____

_____

2. Turn your main idea into your topic sentence. Be sure to repeat some key words from the question in your topic sentence.

   Write your topic sentence here.

_____

_____

_____

3. Review the list of people and descriptive details from the poem (number 4 of Step 2) and the list of details that you created (number 11 of Step 2).

   Place a check mark ✔ next to the details in both lists that you want to use.

   Number the details that you selected in the order in which you want to use them.

4. **Now write your answer.**

_____

_____

_____

_____

_____

_____

_____

_____

_____

_____

_____

_____

_____

_____

 HINT: _When you write about your own opinion, use phrases such as_ I think, I believe, _and_ in my opinion. _These phrases signal to your reader that you are giving your opinion and not someone else's, or stating a fact._

STEP 4

ASSESS *what you have written.*

How do you think your answer measures up to the rubric?

4 =   I respond clearly, completely, and accurately to the question.
I include a topic sentence that repeats key words from the question.
I explain my opinion with details—my own and ones from the poem.
I present a well-organized answer. Planning is evident.
I use transitions to make my answer read more smoothly.
I use complete, correct sentences.

3 =   I respond to the question accurately, but not clearly.
I include a topic sentence.
I include some supporting details—my own and ones from the poem.
I present an organized answer.
I use some transitions.
I use complete, correct sentences.

2 =   I answer the question, but not completely or clearly.
I do not have a topic sentence.
I include a few supporting details from the poem, but none of my own.
I do not use transitions.
I do not use complete and correct sentences.

1 =   I do not respond appropriately to the question.
I do not have a topic sentence.
I include few details, and many are not relevant.
My answer is disorganized. Little or no planning is evident.
I do not use transitions.
I do not use complete and correct sentences.

How does your answer compare to the rubric? Before you decide, take a look at Minh's answer that earned a "4." Pay particular attention to how Minh blends his own ideas with examples from the poem into his answer.

157

I think that Walt Whitman sees America as a strong nation made up of many different people. Each person sings a different song because each person is different. Whitman calls the songs "varied carols." Examples are "The boatman singing what belongs to him in his boat" and "The shoemaker singing as he sits on his bench."

Because the poet does not list all the people in our country, I think that the ones he lists represent the average citizen. These average citizens work hard for the good of the country. The citizens of our country are "Singing, with open mouths, their strong melodious song." Also, as they sing their individual songs, they all come together in a harmony that makes America a great and strong country.

Moreover, I think there is more to this poem than people singing songs. The songs are not really songs. They represent the voices and opinions of the people of our country. Everyone has the right to sing out loud, which means to speak. You are not silenced because you are different. Whitman has created a picture of proud individuals who are happy and productive. He celebrates the greatness of democracy and America.

What would an evaluator say about Minh's answer?
- He must have read the question carefully because he answers it completely, clearly, and accurately.
- He states his opinion and repeats some of the key words from the question in his topic sentence.
- He supports his opinion with his own ideas and details from the poem.
- He uses transitions to make his answer read more smoothly.
- He writes complete sentences.

Let's examine Minh's answer to see why it merits a "4."

1. Minh repeats some of the key words from the question in his topic sentence.

   Write his topic sentence here.

   _____

   _____

2. Minh quotes from the poem in his explanation.

   Write one of the quotations here.

   _____

   _____

3. Minh uses his own ideas to support his opinion.

   Write two sentences that use Minh's own ideas.

   _____

   _____

   _____

   _____

Minh uses transitions to move from one idea to the next in his answer. This makes his answer read more smoothly. Additional-information words are transitions that can be useful when explaining an opinion.

Skill: Using Additional-Information Words

Additional-information words signal to the reader that a new idea is coming up. They help the reader to focus on the new material.

Additional-Information Words

also	along with	besides
additionally	another	for example
in addition	as well as	for instance
moreover		

4. Find the three additional-information transitions that Minh uses in his answer.

    Write them here.

    _____

Did you include in your answer any transitions that show the addition of information? Did you include any transitions at all? When you revise your answer, think about adding transitions. They can make your writing easier to read and understand.

Now let's take a look at your answer.

5. Did you include your opinion and repeat some key words from the question in your topic sentence?

    If not, revise your topic sentence here.

    _____

    _____

    _____

6. Did you include examples from the poem to support your opinion?

   If not, write some examples from the poem that you might include.

   _____

   _____

   _____

   _____

   _____

7. Did you include your own ideas to support your opinion? If not, what ideas could you add to make your opinion stronger?

   Write your ideas here.

   _____

   _____

   _____

   _____

   _____

8. Would adding some transitions make your answer easier to read and understand?

   Circle any places where you could add transitions when you revise your answer.

9. Did you include any sentence fragments or run-on sentences?

   Underline any fragments or run-ons.

   Correct those sentences here.

   _____

   _____

   _____

   _____

10. Would your answer read more smoothly if you combined some sentences?

    Put brackets around sentences that you could combine in your revision.

STEP 5 IMPROVE *your answer.*

1. Think about the ideas you have written about your answer.

2. Read the rubric on page 157 again. Think about your answer and about the description of a "4" paper.

3. **Use your new ideas to revise and rewrite your answer.**

_____

_____

_____

_____

_____

_____

_____

_____

_____

_____

_____

_____

_____

_____

_____

Remember to review the "One Last Look" questions below.

ONE LAST LOOK

Did you
- ❏ answer the question that was asked?
- ❏ state your opinion in your topic sentence?
- ❏ include details to support your opinion?
- ❏ write complete sentences?
- ❏ fill all or most of the answer lines?
- ❏ check your spelling and punctuation?

Lesson 9

Persuading the Reader

You spend a great deal of your time trying to persuade people to do things, or being persuaded yourself to do something. For example, you may try to persuade your parents to let you watch more TV or to stay out later. You may try to persuade your teachers to give you more time to complete an assignment, or to assign less homework. At the same time, you are the target of persuasive efforts by others. Ads try to get you to watch certain programs, buy certain products, or support certain candidates or issues. Even the president of the United States in his State of the Union Address wants to persuade you to support his agenda.

To **persuade** is to convince others to accept your point of view or to do what you want them to do. A test question may ask you to take a position on an issue and write

- a persuasive essay.
- a letter to an editor.
- an editorial.
- a speech.

Regardless of the product you must write, your goal is to convince your audience to agree with the facts you present, share your opinion, and, finally, accept your conclusion.

In this lesson you will write a letter to the editor to persuade the newspaper's readers to accept your point of view about an issue. In preparing your letter, you must

 ✔ introduce the topic of your letter in the first paragraph.
 ✔ inform readers of your opinion in the first paragraph.
 ✔ develop the body of your letter by focusing on three main points, or arguments.
 ✔ restate your main idea in your conclusion.
 ✔ ask readers to take the action you are requesting.

To develop and support your point of view, you will need **arguments**. These are reasons that explain your point of view. Arguments should be based on facts, not opinions.

Facts:	Opinions:
• are generally accepted as true. • can be checked for accuracy. • can be proven to be true.	• are beliefs. • cannot be checked for accuracy. • are neither right nor wrong. • should be based on facts, but are not facts.

An opinion is the conclusion a person reaches after analyzing the facts of an issue.

This lesson does not provide an open-ended question based on a reading. Instead, you will respond to a prompt that sets up a situation by explaining background for the writing topic. The second part of the prompt gives directions about what you are to write. Be sure to read the entire prompt carefully.

Specific words are words that name a person or thing, or describe an action. Using specific words will make your writing just that—more specific. They will give your writing relevancy and directness by naming and describing people, places, things, and actions.

In this Lesson, you will learn how to...

- write a persuasive letter to the editor.
- use specific words to make your writing more interesting.

STEP 1

READ *the question thoughtfully.*

Read the question carefully.

Many of the parents at your school are concerned with the amount of time their children spend nightly doing homework. Some parents have started a campaign to limit the homework that teachers can assign to students. Teachers at your school do not agree with this campaign. They state that homework is necessary to learning because doing homework enables students to practice what they are learning.

What do you think? Write a letter to the editor of your local newspaper stating your position. Support your position with convincing arguments. Begin your letter with "Dear Editor:".

1. What does the question ask you to do?

   Underline the parts of the question that tell you what to do. These are your key words.

2. **Write those key words here.**

   _____

   _____

3. Are you sure you know what to write about?

   Restate in your own words what the question asks you to do.

   _____

   _____

   _____

STEP 2 **THINK**

THINK about what the question asks you to do.

1. **Write the key words from the prompt here.**

   _____

   _____

2. What is the topic of your letter?

   Write your topic here.

   _____

   _____

3. What is your point of view about the issue? Do you think homework should be limited or not?

   Write your point of view here.

   _____

   _____

   _____

   _____

HINT: *Where do you find facts to support your opinion and develop your arguments? You look at your own experience and the experiences of others. You ask yourself questions to start your thinking about the topic.*

4. What ideas can you think of to help support your point of view? What questions can you ask yourself about the topic of homework? Here are some questions to get you started:

Place a checkmark next to any questions that you can answer.

- Does your school have a homework policy?
- If it does, why did it establish a specific policy?
- What is the policy?
- Is it considered successful by the teachers? Students? Parents?
- Do you know anyone whose school has a specific homework policy?
- Do you know why it was started?
- Do you know if it is successful?

Write answers to the questions that you placed checkmarks next to.

_____

_____

_____

_____

_____

_____

_____

_____

5. If you could answer few questions in number 4, don't give up. Think about the amount of homework you actually have.

   Write your ideas in response to each of the questions below.

   a. Does it keep you from joining after-school activities?

   _____

   b. Does it keep you from taking an after-school job?

   _____

   c. Does it keep you up at night?

   _____

   d. Are you ever unable to finish it all because you have to work after school?

   _____

   e. How would setting up a schoolwide homework policy affect you?

   _____

These are the points, or arguments, you can make to support your point of view.

6. To make your letter more interesting and to describe your arguments in greater depth, you will need supporting details.

   Write details related to each argument in number 5.

   a. _____

   b. _____

   c. _____

   d. _____

   e. _____

STEP 3 — WRITE

1. What is the main idea of your letter?

   Write your main idea here.

   _____

   _____

2. How will you introduce the main idea?

   Write your topic sentence here.

   _____

   _____

   _____

HINT: *A letter is like any other piece of writing. It needs a topic sentence to state your main idea.*

3. How are you going to state your point of view?

   Write the statement of your point of view here.

   _____

   _____

   _____

4. Which three arguments are you going to develop in your speech?

   Circle three ideas in number 5 of Step 2 that you want to use.

5. Which details will you need to support each argument?

   Circle the relevant details in number 6 of Step 2.

6. **Number the ideas and details in the order in which you want to use them.**

7. **Now write your letter.**

_____

_____

_____

_____

_____

_____

_____

_____

_____

_____

_____

_____

_____

_____

_____

_____

_____

_____

_____

_____

_____

HINT: *Remember to end your letter like this:*
Sincerely yours,
[your name]
[your grade, your school name]

STEP
4

ASSESS *what you have written.*

Like any other piece of writing, a letter can be evaluated for organization, content, sentence structure, word choice, and standard English. Apply the following rubric to your letter to see how it measures up.

4 =   I respond clearly and completely to the prompt.
       I include a topic sentence that repeats key words from the question.
       I state my opinion clearly near the beginning of the letter.
       I include three reasons, or facts, to support my point of view.
       I include supporting evidence for each reason.
       I conclude with a restatement of my main idea and a call to action.
       I present a well-organized answer. Planning is evident.
       I use complete sentences.
       I have no errors in standard English.

3 =   I respond to the prompt clearly.
       I include a topic sentence.
       I state my opinion near the beginning of the letter.
       I include three reasons, or facts, to support my point of view.
       I include some supporting details.
       I do not present a conclusion.
       Most of my answer is organized.
       I use complete sentences.
       I have no errors in standard English.

174

2 =   I respond to the prompt somewhat.
I do not have a topic sentence.
I do not state my opinion clearly.
I include only one reason, or fact, to support my point of view.
I include many unnecessary details.
I do not present a conclusion.
My answer is disorganized.
I use many incomplete sentences.
I make numerous errors in standard English.

1 =   I do not respond to the prompt.
I do not have a topic sentence.
I do not state my opinion clearly.
I include only one reason.
I include details that do not relate to my opinion.
I do not present a conclusion.
I have written a disorganized answer. No planning is evident.
I use many incomplete sentences.
I have numerous errors in standard English.

How does your answer compare to the rubric? Before you decide, take a look at Reynosha's answer. It merits a "4."

Dear Editor:

The amount of time spent on homework is an issue at Wood High School. I absolutely agree with those who say there is too much homework being assigned.

It has been reported that some students have four to five hours of homework each night. These same students complain that they often do not get to bed until after midnight. I am one of these students. Do the math! If a student is in school for six hours and has four to five hours of homework a night, that's ten to eleven hours of work a day. An adult working ten to eleven hours a day would be moaning and groaning about the awful workload.

Some students have been forced to quit their after-school activities or their after-school jobs because of the tons of homework assigned to them. Students are losing sleep, being overworked, eliminating after-school activities, and forgoing jobs because of the extraordinary amount of homework.

We all agree—even students—that homework is an important part of learning. The teachers are right. However, homework is being piled on every night. I did some research on education Web sites and I found that whatever grade a person is in, multiply that grade by ten and that is how much time we should spend on homework. Thus, a tenth-grader should receive no more than 100 minutes of homework a night.

We students are being assigned too much homework every day. A homework policy that is reasonable will eliminate the problem. I urge the school administration to adopt a policy that limits homework.

Sincerely,

Reynosha Taylor

Junior, Wood High School

What would an evaluator say about Reynosha's answer?

✔ She must have read the question carefully because she answers it clearly and completely.

✔ She repeats some of the key words in her topic sentence.

✔ She clearly states her opinion near the beginning of the letter.

✔ She includes three reasons, or facts.

✔ She supports her reasons with details.

✔ She restates her main idea and calls for action.

✔ She writes complete sentences.

Let's examine Reynosha's answer to see why it merits a "4."

1. Reynosha repeats some of the key words from the question in her topic sentence.

   Write her topic sentence here.

   _____

   _____

2. How does Reynosha state her opinion?

   Write that sentence here.

   _____

   _____

3. She gives three arguments for establishing a homework policy.

   Write Reynosha's three arguments here.

   _____

   _____

   _____

   _____

   _____

4. Reynosha gives details, or evidence, to support and explain her arguments.

   Write two pieces of evidence that she uses.

   _____

   _____

   _____

   _____

5. She asks the school administration to take action.

   Write the action she wants the administration to take.

   _____

   _____

6. She restates her main idea in her conclusion.

   Write the restatement of her main idea here.

   _____

   _____

One reason that Reynosha's answer scores a "4" is her use of specific words.

Skill: Using Specific Words

Specific words are also called concrete words. They name a person, place, or thing, or they describe an action. Actions verbs and vivid adjectives are two types of specific words that add life and color to your writing. Specific words also make your writing stronger.

7a. In her first draft, Reynosha wrote:

They also say they get to bed late.

Write Reynosha's revised sentence that uses more specific language.

_____

_____

7b. In her first draft, Reynosha wrote:

Anyone working ten to eleven hours a day would complain.

Write Reynosha's revised sentence that uses more specific language.

_____

_____

7c. Reynosha ended her first draft with this call to action:

It is time to solve this problem.

Write the sentence that Reynosha uses to end her final draft.

_____

_____

In revising your answer, think about your word choices. Are there any verbs or adjectives that could be replaced with more specific words to make your answer more interesting to the reader?

Now let's take a look at your answer.

8. Did you repeat some of the key words from the question in your topic sentence?

    If not, revise your topic sentence here.

    _____

    _____

    _____

9. In what sentence did you state your opinion?

    Write that sentence here.

    _____

    _____

    _____

10. How many arguments did you use in your letter to support your opinion?

    Write the number here. _____

11. If you used fewer than three, think of additional arguments to include in your revision.

    Write your additional arguments here.

    _____

    _____

    _____

    _____

12. What evidence, or details, did you use to support your arguments?

    Write one piece of evidence here.

    _____

    _____

13. How did you ask the school administration to take action?

Write that sentence here.

_____

_____

14. Would your letter be stronger if you replaced some words with more specific, concrete words? Go back and check your letter.

Circle words that you could replace with stronger ones.

15. Check to see that there are no fragments or run-on sentences in your answer.

Put brackets around any sentence fragments or run-ons.
Revise them when you revise your answer.

STEP
5

IMPROVE *your answer.*

1. Think about the ideas you wrote when you assessed your answer.

2. Read the rubric on pages 174–175 again. Think about your answer and about the description of a "4" paper.

3. **Use your new ideas to revise and rewrite your answer.**

_____

_____

_____

_____

_____

_____

_____

_____

_____

_____

_____

_____

_____

_____

_____

_____

_____

_____

_____

_____

_____

_____

_____

_____

Remember to review the "One Last Look" questions below.

ONE LAST *LOOK*

Did you
- ❏ answer the question that was asked?
- ❏ follow the format for a persuasive letter—introduction, development, and conclusion, including a call to action?
- ❏ include details that support your arguments?
- ❏ write complete sentences?
- ❏ fill all or most of the answer lines?
- ❏ check your spelling and punctuation?

Testing Yourself

The purpose of practicing the 5 steps of the smart way to answer open-ended questions is to make them automatic for you. The idea is that as soon as you read an open-ended question, you begin to apply the 5 steps. You should

- **read** and underline the key words in the question.
- **think** about what the reading says, and what the question asks you to do.
- organize your ideas and **write**.
- **assess** your answer in relation to the question and the reading.
- revise and **improve** your answer.

If the question has no reading, you can still follow the same 5 steps. In this case, you don't gather information from a reading. Instead, you use your own ideas, experiences, and opinions to write your answer. The steps are still important. You need to organize your own thoughts the same way you organize information from someone else's writing.

You have been learning and using the 5 steps in Part A of this book. In Part B, you will be able to practice the 5 steps on your own. This part is made up of 6 self-tests. The first three self-tests are based on a reading. The last three self-tests are prompts that are not based on readings. Like all the questions in this book, they are modeled after real test questions.

You have worked hard in this book learning and practicing the 5 steps. Now you can use this knowledge to answer any open-ended question on any test.

Remember:
Read • Think • Write • Assess • Improve

THE WORLD OF ANIMATION

I was very lucky last summer. I was part of a special summer program at the local university. It was a two-week exploration of different kinds of science. We had a physics class every morning, and in the afternoon we had different kinds of activities. The first week we built and programmed robots. We were supposed to see how many different tasks the robots could do. The camp record was 170 tasks. My partner, Liu, and I got our robot to do 10 tasks before it fell over. The record holder wasn't in any danger from us. We also took a boat trip and learned about plankton, the tiny animals that bigger fish feed on. We picked up mud from the ocean bottom and caught a bat ray, too.

The most interesting session, however, was held in the darkened auditorium. That was the afternoon that Danielle Feinburg came to talk to us. Danielle is not widely known, but she is a very important person in the world of animation. She has done the lighting in feature-length animated movies.

In her speech, Danielle told us how an animated movie is made. The first thing she did was show us a picture of a graph with a rectangular prism rising out of it. Unlike in a live-action movie, in which you film a real landscape, or background, you have to create the landscape in an animated movie. So this little rectangle on the graph was a piece of that landscape.

The rectangle turned out to be a table leg. Danielle explained how the animation process works. She said, for example, that the creator of the table leg would go to the director and say, "Look, director! Look! I have created that wonderful table leg you told me to draw." The director would look at the leg and exclaim that it needs more detail in the shape. It needs to be carved, not plain. After all, why is the audience going to like a plain table leg?

So the artist goes back to the computer and creates a much more unique and exciting table leg. Then the artist goes back to the director to get it approved. When it is approved, the artist makes four table legs. Each one is exactly the same as the first one. The artist sends the legs up to the next department along with the table top.

Then this department makes the table more explicit. Danielle explained that this means an artist makes it look more like a real table. He or she adds grain to the wood and makes the table look polished and shiny. Then *this artist* goes to the director and says, "Hey! Look at this nice table I have set up for you. I even got that special kind of wood you wanted!" The director looks at the table and says, "Yeah, it's wonderful, but we want to make it look as if this table has been used for a long time."

So the artist takes it back and makes it look old. A little bit of wear is added here, and maybe a crack or two goes there. The artist takes the drawing of the table back to the director. The director is very pleased with what the artist has done and sends it to the next department.

In this department, the people are called producers. They take all the separate pieces that have come from the other departments and make everything look like a room. Let's say that they are making a living room. They have a couch, television, coffee table, some chairs, a couple of plants, and some books and magazines. The producers put them together so that they look just like a living room. Yet the director is still not pleased. "You're building a normal family's living room," he says to the producers. "This looks like a room in Buckingham Palace."

The producers sigh and go back to their computers to make it look like a "normal" living room. They put dust on the television and flatten the pillows on the couch. They leave an open book on the coffee table along with a half-filled glass of water. A few pieces of crumpled paper appear on the table. Doing things like this makes it seem as though people actually live in this room. "The first room that the producers presented seemed as though the owner of the room had a maid who tidied up all the time," Danielle said.

The producers show the "normal" room to the director. Once it is approved, it is time to add the people. So the character designers create all the people that the script calls for to be in that room at that time. Let's say that five people are supposed to be in this living room waiting for someone to arrive. The people have to be doing something while they are waiting. When the designers first put the characters in the room, however, they are just trying to figure out where all of the people should be. So the designers draw some sitting on the couches and others standing up.

The designers look at the scene and decide that it does not look too exciting. At the moment, all they have is a group of straight-backed people who either sit staring blankly ahead, or stand up staring blankly ahead. So the designers redraw the people to look relaxed. The ones on the couch are redrawn to seem to be talking to each other. One of the standing people is reading the newspaper over the shoulder of another person who is standing. The other two standing people are laughing over some imaginary joke. Now, the room looks more real. All of the people are doing something.

Once the scene and the characters are drawn, the animators make the magic happen. The camera rolls and the people speak to each other and move around the room in realistic ways. "Remember that every inch of that screen is animation," Danielle explained. Every inch had to be created. Even the little pieces of useless-looking paper on the coffee table play an important part in making the scene realistic. After Danielle finished her illustrated talk, I understood how complicated animation is. I'll never look at an animated movie the same way again.

Self-Test 1. *Identifying the Main Idea and Supporting Details*

Why is "The World of Animation" a good title for this selection? Explain your answer by using relevant information from the article.

_____

_____

_____

_____

_____

_____

_____

_____

_____

_____

_____

_____

_____

_____

_____

Use the following rubric to assess your answer.

4 =   I answer the question clearly, completely, and accurately.
       I state the main idea clearly and accurately.
       I state details clearly, and they support the main idea.
       I use transitions to help my writing flow easily from sentence to sentence.
       My writing is interesting because I use description and specific words.
       I use complete, correct sentences.

3 =   I answer the question accurately but not completely.
       I state the main idea clearly and accurately.
       I state details that for the most part support the main idea.
       I use only a few transitions.
       I use some specific words and description, so my writing is somewhat
          interesting.
       I use complete, correct sentences.

2 =   I do not answer the question completely.
       I state the main idea but not clearly or accurately.
       Most of the details that I use do not support the main idea.
       I do not use any transitions.
       I use a few specific words but no descriptive details.
       Most of the sentences I use are complete sentences.
       I make numerous errors in standard English.

1 =   I do not answer the question.
       I do not state the main idea.
       I do not clearly state details. Most details do not support the main idea.
       I do not use transitions.
       I do not use specific words or descriptive details.
       I use incomplete, incorrect sentences.

What score do you give your answer? _____

How can you improve your writing? **On separate sheets of paper, use the 5 smart steps to revise your answer.**

Self-Test 2. *Explaining Steps in a Process*

 The editor of your school newspaper has asked you to write an article about how an animated film is made. Use relevant information from the reading to write your article.

_____

_____

_____

_____

_____

_____

_____

_____

_____

_____

_____

_____

Use the following rubric to assess your answer.

4 = I answer the question clearly, completely, and accurately.

I state the main idea clearly and accurately.

I state details clearly, and they support the main idea.

I use transitions to help my writing flow easily from sentence to sentence.

My writing is interesting because I use description and specific words.

I use complete, correct sentences.

3 = I answer the question accurately but not completely.

I state the main idea clearly and accurately.

I state details that for the most part support the main idea.

I use only a few transitions.

I use some specific words and description, so my writing is somewhat interesting.

I use complete, correct sentences.

2 = I do not answer the question completely.

I state the main idea but not clearly or accurately.

Most of the details that I use do not support the main idea.

I do not use any transitions.

I use a few specific words but no descriptive details.

Most of the sentences I use are complete sentences.

I make numerous errors in standard English.

1 = I do not answer the question.

I do not state the main idea.

I do not clearly state details. Most details do not support the main idea.

I do not use transitions.

I do not use specific words or descriptive details.

I use incomplete, incorrect sentences.

What score do you give your answer? _____

How can you improve your writing? **On separate sheets of paper, use the 5 smart steps to revise your answer.**

Self-Test 3. *Identifying and Describing a Personal Experience*

 The narrator of the story is very excited about meeting Danielle Feinburg and hearing about her work. Think of a time when you were particularly excited about hearing someone speak, meeting someone, or watching someone perform. Describe this experience. Use vivid words to capture the excitement you felt during this experience.

_____

_____

_____

_____

_____

_____

_____

_____

_____

_____

_____

_____

Use the following rubric to assess your answer.

4 = I answer the question clearly, completely, and accurately.
I state the main idea clearly and accurately.
I state details clearly, and they support the main idea.
I use transitions to help my writing flow easily from sentence to sentence.
My writing is interesting because I use description and specific words.
I use complete, correct sentences.

3 = I answer the question accurately but not completely.
I state the main idea clearly and accurately.
I state details that for the most part support the main idea.
I use only a few transitions.
I use some specific words and description, so my writing is somewhat interesting.
I use complete, correct sentences.

2 = I do not answer the question completely.
I state the main idea but not clearly or accurately.
Most of the details that I use do not support the main idea.
I do not use any transitions.
I use a few specific words but no descriptive details.
Most of the sentences I use are complete sentences.
I make numerous errors in standard English.

1 = I do not answer the question.
I do not state the main idea.
I do not clearly state details. Most details do not support the main idea.
I do not use transitions.
I do not use specific words or descriptive details.
I use incomplete, incorrect sentences.

What score do you give your answer? _____

How can you improve your writing? **On separate sheets of paper, use the 5 smart steps to revise your answer.**

Self-Test 4. *Expressing Your Opinion*

The difference between what one expects to happen and what actually happens is often an element in a work of literature. This unexpected result is called irony. Irony is something that happens that is inconsistent with what might be expected to happen, especially when the result is absurd or laughable.

Select a work of literature—a short story or a novel—that you have read in or out of school in which there is a difference between what is expected and what actually happens. Think of a story with a twist. Write an essay to explain the situation and why it is an example of irony.

_____

_____

_____

_____

_____

_____

_____

_____

_____

Use the following rubric to assess your answer.

4 = I answer the question clearly, completely, and accurately.
I state the main idea clearly and accurately.
I state details clearly, and they support the main idea.
I use transitions to help my writing flow easily from sentence to sentence.
My writing is interesting because I use description and specific words.
I use complete, correct sentences.

3 = I answer the question accurately but not completely.
I state the main idea clearly and accurately.
I state details that for the most part support the main idea.
I use only a few transitions.
I use some specific words and description, so my writing is somewhat interesting.
I use complete, correct sentences.

2 = I do not answer the question completely.
I state the main idea but not clearly or accurately.
Most of the details that I use do not support the main idea.
I do not use any transitions.
I use a few specific words but no descriptive details.
Most of the sentences I use are complete sentences.
I make numerous errors in standard English.

1 = I do not answer the question.
I do not state the main idea.
I do not clearly state details. Most details do not support the main idea.
I do not use transitions.
I do not use specific words or descriptive details.
I use incomplete, incorrect sentences.

What score do you give your answer? _____

How can you improve your writing? **On separate sheets of paper, use the 5 smart steps to revise your answer.**

Self-Test 5. *Writing a Persuasive Letter*

Some parents have urged your school district to take an active role in better nutrition for students. The subject came up repeatedly at a local school board meeting. In the spirit of helping students use the nutrition information they learn in their health classes, some parents suggested better balanced menus in the school cafeterias.

The Director of School Food Services has gone one step further. She has suggested that ice cream, soft drinks, and other sweets be removed from the cafeterias and vending machines. She suggested that soft drinks in the vending machines be replaced with juice drinks. Write a letter to the director in which you agree or disagree with her proposal. Support your opinion with reasons.

Use the following rubric to assess your answer.

4 = I answer the question clearly, completely, and accurately.
I state the main idea clearly and accurately.
I state details clearly, and they support the main idea.
I use transitions to help my writing flow easily from sentence to sentence.
My writing is interesting because I use description and specific words.
I use complete, correct sentences.

3 = I answer the question accurately but not completely.
I state the main idea clearly and accurately.
I state details that for the most part support the main idea.
I use only a few transitions.
I use some specific words and description, so my writing is somewhat interesting.
I use complete, correct sentences.

2 = I do not answer the question completely.
I state the main idea but not clearly or accurately.
Most of the details that I use do not support the main idea.
I do not use any transitions.
I use a few specific words but no descriptive details.
Most of the sentences I use are complete sentences.
I make numerous errors in standard English.

1 = I do not answer the question.
I do not state the main idea.
I do not clearly state details. Most details do not support the main idea.
I do not use transitions.
I do not use specific words or descriptive details.
I use incomplete, incorrect sentences.

What score do you give your answer? _____

How can you improve your writing? **On separate sheets of paper, use the 5 smart steps to revise your answer.**

Self-Test 6. *Explaining Cause and Effect*

Each day, we come into contact with many people—family, friends, teachers, coaches, and neighbors. We read about people in the news, on television, and in the movies. We meet characters in the books we read. Think about someone who has made an impression on you or has influenced you in some way.

Write an essay identifying this person and explaining how he or she has influenced you.

Use the following rubric to assess your answer.

4 = I answer the question clearly, completely, and accurately.
I state the main idea clearly and accurately.
I state details clearly, and they support the main idea.
I use transitions to help my writing flow easily from sentence to sentence.
My writing is interesting because I use description and specific words.
I use complete, correct sentences.

3 = I answer the question accurately but not completely.
I state the main idea clearly and accurately.
I state details that for the most part support the main idea.
I use only a few transitions.
I use some specific words and description, so my writing is somewhat interesting.
I use complete, correct sentences.

2 = I do not answer the question completely.
I state the main idea but not clearly or accurately.
Most of the details that I use do not support the main idea.
I do not use any transitions.
I use a few specific words but no descriptive details.
Most of the sentences I use are complete sentences.
I make numerous errors in standard English.

1 = I do not answer the question.
I do not state the main idea.
I do not clearly state details. Most details do not support the main idea.
I do not use transitions.
I do not use specific words or descriptive details.
I use incomplete, incorrect sentences.

What score do you give your answer? _____

How can you improve your writing? **On separate sheets of paper, use the 5 smart steps to revise your answer.**